New educational landscapes: innovative perspectives in language learning and technology

Edited by Alessia Plutino, Kate Borthwick, and Erika Corradini

Research-publishing.net

R esearch-publishing.net

Published by Research-publishing.net, a not-for-profit association
Voillans, France, info@research-publishing.net

New educational landscapes: innovative perspectives in language learning and technology
Edited by Alessia Plutino, Kate Borthwick, and Erika Corradini

Publication date: 2019/07/10

Typeset by Research-publishing.net
Cover design by © Raphaël Savina (raphael@savina.net)

ISBN13: 978-2-490057-48-1 (Ebook, PDF, colour)
ISBN13: 978-2-490057-49-8 (Ebook, EPUB, colour)
ISBN13: 978-2-490057-47-4 (Paperback - Print on demand, black and white)
Print on demand technology is a high-quality, innovative and ecological printing method; with which the book is never 'out of stock' or 'out of print'.

British Library Cataloguing-in-Publication Data.
A cataloguing record for this book is available from the British Library.

Legal deposit, UK: British Library.
Legal deposit, France: Bibliothèque Nationale de France - Dépôt légal: juillet 2019.

Table of contents

v   Notes on contributors

1   Introduction – symposium short papers
     Alessia Plutino, Kate Borthwick, and Erika Corradini

5   Multilingual immersive communication technology: repurposing virtual
     reality for Italian teaching
     *Billy Brick, Tiziana Cervi-Wilson, Sean Graham, Tsvetan Tsankov,
     Michael Loizou, Nina Godson, and Kelly Ryan*

11   A study on technology-based speech assistants
     Serpil Meri-Yilan

19   Vocabulary Kingdom: gamified EAP vocabulary acquisition using
     blended learning
     Christina Markanastasakis

25   MISSION BERLIN – a mobile gamified exploration of a new
     educational landscape
     Bart Pardoel, Salomi Papadima-Sophocleous, and Androulla Athanasiou

33   A deep linguistic computer-assisted language learning game for Italian
     Jessica Zipf

41   Using online volunteer translation communities for language learning
     in formal education
     Anna Comas-Quinn

47   BMELTET – Blending MOOCs into English language teacher education
     with telecollaboration
     Marina Orsini-Jones and Abraham Cerveró Carrascosa

55   Design recommendations to address cultural issues in multicultural
     MOOCs: a systematic literature review
     Rana Shahini, Hugh C. Davis, and Kate Borthwick

63   The lights and shadows of intercultural exchange projects for 21st-century
     skills development: analysis and comparison of two online case studies
     Marta Fondo and Pedro Jacobetty

Table of contents

71 Telecollaboration in the foundation year classroom: the 'Global Student Collective'
Lucy Watson

77 What I did on my holidays: digital fieldtrips and digital literacies
Sarah Fielding

85 "What is this place?" – using screencasts to guide international students around the virtual learning environment
Michael Salmon

91 Author index

Notes on contributors

1.   Editors/reviewers

Alessia Plutino is Senior Teaching Fellow in Italian at the University of Southampton and also Associate Lecturer of Italian at the Open University. Her areas of interest are on material design, CALL – particularly with regards to student independent learning skills and aspects of cultural and intercultural awareness integrated into language teaching; collaborative learning via social media and VR. From January 2019, she is conference chair of the e-Learning Symposium, which runs annually at the University of Southampton.

Kate Borthwick is Principal Enterprise Fellow (educational innovation) in Modern Languages and Linguistics at the University of Southampton. She leads the University's MOOC programme as Director of Programme Development (online ed) in the Digital Learning team. She is an award-winning, experienced language teacher, developer of online learning materials/courses, and e-tutor. She was involved in the creation of two repositories of OERs: LanguageBox and HumBox. She is course designer for four FutureLearn/UoS MOOCs. She was conference chair for the annual EuroCALL conference, 2017 (European Association for Computer Assisted Language Learning), and was elected onto the executive board of EuroCALL in 2018.

Erika Corradini is Senior Teaching Fellow in Academic Development in the Centre for Higher Education Practice, University of Southampton. Her background is in education development in the areas of languages and linguistics. After completing her PhD in English, Erika worked as lecturer in Humanities and later moved into education development and academic support. In her career so far, Erika has created and led projects centred on the professional development of teaching staff in the secondary and tertiary education sectors. This has involved the creation of education enhancement activities for fostering good academic practice in teaching and learning, including but not limited to e-learning, cross-sector partnerships, PGRs, and educators' training, as well as promotion of the teaching profession in the UK and beyond.

2.　Authors

Androulla Athanasiou is English Language Instructor at the Language Centre of the Cyprus University of Technology. She holds an MA in English and Language Studies and Methods, an MA in Educational Leadership, and a PhD in English Language Teaching. Her research interests focus on material design, CALL, learner autonomy, collaborative learning, and CEFR.

Billy Brick is Languages Centre Manager in the School of Humanities at Coventry University. He teaches Multimedia in Language Teaching and Learning and Computer Assisted Language Learning and has been involved with numerous JISC/HEA projects. His research interests include virtual reality, social networking sites and language learning, and mobile assisted language learning.

Abraham Cerveró Carrascosa is the Erasmus Coordinator and Lecturer in TEFL and Linguistics at Florida Universitària in València, Spain. He has contributed to national and international conferences and published work on teacher education, CALL, and multilingual policies and intercultural practices in primary, secondary, and higher education.

Tiziana Cervi-Wilson is Senior Lecturer and the Coordinator for the UWLP and career and employability modules in the School of Humanities at Coventry University. She teaches Italian modules at all levels. She is interested in language learning and teaching, digital literacy, multimedia, and computer and mobile assisted language learning. She has presented various papers regarding language learning and technology and has been involved in different HEA projects.

Anna Comas-Quinn is Senior Lecturer at the School of Languages and Applied Linguistics at The Open University, UK. She researches technology-enhanced language learning, teacher development and open education, and currently investigates the potential of online volunteer translation to extend open practice in the teaching of languages and translation.

Hugh C. Davis is Professor of Learning Technologies at the University of Southampton. Hugh has a long history of research in Hypertext and in Learning Technologies, with over 250 publications in these areas and more than 35 grants. He also has significant experience as an educational change-agent in HE at both a local and national level, and until stepping down in April 2016, was director of the Institute of Learning Innovation and Development. His current interests include the 'virtual university', learning at scale (MOOCs), and how the web changes HE and learning, all of which fall under web science.

Dr Sarah Fielding is Learning Designer in the University of Southampton's Digital Learning Team. She has a PhD in Earth Sciences and previously worked in Learning Support, Outreach, and Science Communication. Sarah has particular interests in virtual and augmented reality, and has produced UoS massive online open courses.

Marta Fondo is Research Assistant, PhD candidate, and Designer and Coordinator of Virtual Exchange (VE) projects at the ICT and Education department at the Universitat Oberta de Catalunya. Her areas of interest are the intercultural and emotional factors involved in learning, teaching, and communicating in the foreign language, CLIL, CMC, and VE.

Nina Godson is Assistant Professor at Coventry University. Nina has developed e-learning resources on infection control and Cardiopulmonary Resuscitation. Previous projects include the Immersive Community Communication projects through the use of oculus rift glasses to promote communication amongst pre-registration healthcare professionals

Sean Graham is Learning Technologist with a specific remit for research. He has led a number of high profile VR and AR applications, gaining broadsheet and terrestrial media exposure for his advancement in mixed-reality environments. Currently studying a part-time MA in animation and illustration. His research interests pertain to immersive technology, the human relationship with virtual characters, and the use of new media in narrative form.

Pedro Jacobetty is a researcher working on the relationship between digital technologies and society. He holds a PhD from the Open University of Catalonia (IN3-UOC) and a BS and MRes in Sociology from the University Institute of Lisbon. His main research interests are related to technology, culture, knowledge, power relations, and media and communication.

Michael Loizou is Research Fellow at Coventry University's Disruptive Media Learning Lab. His research interests lie in the fields of using serious games for education, artificial intelligence, incorporating emotional capabilities into virtual agents and using technology in the area of health care.

Christina Markanastasakis has a BA in English Literature from McGill University in Canada, and an MA in Digital Technologies for Language Teaching from Nottingham University in the UK. She has been actively engaged in online and blended learning since 2011, when she began teaching online via Skype. This has enabled her to teach and support students from a variety of countries and remote locations in their quest to communicate more effectively in English, prepare for essential exams, and improve their English for important job interviews. Since 2014, she has taught EAP in various institutions, including Southampton University and the Indonesia Australia Language Foundation. She endeavours to include blended learning methods in class, where students may share and consolidate class material via digital platforms. She believes that the current affordances of Web 2.0 technologies provide a tremendous opportunity for collaboration, connection, and the exchange of ideas which enhance student-centred learning.

Serpil Meri-Yilan is Lecturer in the Department of Interpretation and Translation at AICU in Turkey. She gained her MA in 2011 and PhD in Applied Linguistics for Language Teaching at the University of Southampton in 2017. Her research interests are e-learning, learner autonomy, scaffolding, foreign language learning, humanisation of ELT, digital storytelling, virtual reality, and motivation.

Marina Orsini-Jones is Professor in Education Practice and Associate Head of School (International) in the School of Humanities at Coventry University

(UK). Marina has been involved in e-learning and CALL since 1985 and has published in these fields.

Salomi Papadima-Sophocleous is the Language Centre Director of the Cyprus University of Technology. Amongst other things, she holds a BA in French Language and Literature; an MA in French Literature; an MA in Education; Postgraduate Diplomas in Teaching Methodologies and CALL, and a Doctorate in Applied Linguistics.

Bart Pardoel holds an MA in Computer Assisted Language Learning and a Bachelor of Education degree in German Language and Culture. He teaches German as a Foreign language at a secondary school in the Netherlands. His research interests include materials design, gamification, Moodle, MALL, and game-based language learning.

Kelly Ryan is Lecturer at Coventry University. She currently teaches across the pre-registration Healthcare Education curriculum and is currently Course Director for Return to Nursing and Health Visiting Practice. Publications include pocket survival guide (handbooks) on Cardiopulmonary Resuscitation (co-author: Nina Godson) (2012) and Wound Care (2013) survival published through Routledge.

Michael Salmon is the English for Academic Purposes Coordinator at the University of Liverpool's London campus, where he is responsible for pre-sessional and in-sessional course design. His areas of interest are assessment, blended learning and VLE use, and academic integrity.

Rana Shahini is Lecturer in Educational Technologies section at King Abdul-Aziz University – Jeddah Saudi Arabia, and currently a PhD researcher in The Internet and Web Science Institute in the University of Southampton. Got a BSc degree in Computer Science, MSc in Educational technologies, and another MSc in Web Science and has worked in academia since 2009.

Tsvetan Tsankov is a former BSc Computer Science student, now studying MSc in Data Science and Computational Intelligence. Working at CELE

(Coventry University) as Researcher, he has been involved in the development of several VR and other technology oriented learning resources. Also, he is passionate about the incorporation of educational games for the purpose of making learning more interactive, intuitive, and pleasant for students.

Lucy Watson is Senior Teaching Fellow in the Academic Centre for International Students at the University of Southampton. She is the Programme Leader for the International Foundation Year and specialises in teaching cultural studies and liberal arts. Her research interests include critical pedagogy, global citizenship, and collaborative learning and teaching practices.

Jessica Zipf is a doctoral student in linguistics at the University Konstanz. As her PhD project, she develops a CALL tool for Italian, combining grammar engineering and SLA. Further research interests include theoretical issues of Italian, especially question formation and the interaction between their syntactic structure and information structural content.

Introduction – symposium short papers

Alessia Plutino[1], Kate Borthwick[2], and Erika Corradini[3]

Welcome to this collection of short papers from the eLearning Symposium 2019!

The eLearning Symposium was held on the 25th of January, 2019, at the University of Southampton. It rejoiced in the title 'New Perspectives: elearning symposium rebooted. Language learning and technology in new educational landscapes'. This rather lengthy title worked hard for us: it aimed to capture the hopes and challenges of implementing innovation in language education with technology, as well as the opportunities and risks posed by ongoing change in the educational environments we work in.

It also captured a more personal moment: the rebirth, after a three-year hiatus, of the eLearning Symposium as a community event hosted by Modern Languages and Linguistics (MLL), at the University of Southampton, UK. Until 2016, this event had been organised by the Centre for Languages, Linguistics, and Area Studies (LLAS), an enterprise unit based at Southampton which was itself a reinvention of one of the former Higher Education Academy (HEA) Subject Centres. Over 11 years with LLAS, the symposium had developed to become a focus for the languages community to share knowledge and experience, innovative approaches, and to celebrate language teaching and learning with technology. When LLAS closed in 2016, there was uncertainty over the symposium's future, and we are grateful to MLL at the University of Southampton that they have picked up the mantle!

1. University of Southampton, Southampton, England; a.plutino@soton.ac.uk; https://orcid.org/0000-0001-5552-6753

2. University of Southampton, Southampton, England; k.borthwick@soton.ac.uk; https://orcid.org/0000-0003-2251-7898

3. University of Southampton, Southampton, England; e.corradini@soton.ac.uk; https://orcid.org/0000-0002-6021-150X

How to cite: Plutino, A., Borthwick, K., & Corradini, E. (2019). Introduction – symposium short papers. In A. Plutino, K. Borthwick & E. Corradini (Eds), *New educational landscapes: innovative perspectives in language learning and technology* (pp. 1-4). Research-publishing.net. https://doi.org/10.14705/rpnet.2019.36.948

So in January 2019, the eLearning Symposium was 'rebooted' to engage the languages community again and the event proved to be as inspiring, exciting, and relevant as ever. The eLearning Symposium IS its community – and that community is as innovative, dynamic, and curious about teaching with technology as it ever was. This volume aims to capture a picture of that innovation and enthusiasm and present it to you.

This volume opens with a selection of papers on how educators are exploring the very latest technologies in educational contexts. Billy Brick, Tiziana Cervi-Wilson, and their collaborators describe an experiment with Virtual Reality (VR) for teaching Italian. This pilot saw the repurposing of VR healthcare materials from English and highlights the value and importance of collaborative work between content-creators and linguists in producing high quality language resources. VR technology has the potential for enormous impact on the teaching of language and culture and how we respond as educators will be an important area of research in years to come. Similarly, Serpil Meri-Yilan's study on the value of Speech Recognition Technology (SRT) for teaching speaking skills is a timely one. Such SRT tools are becoming a staple of our daily lives and seem to offer potential for anxiety-free speaking practice. Serpil's study explores some of the benefits and challenges of such tools in education.

A number of papers in this volume consider gamified learning in languages. Language teachers have used games for many years to teach language but the development of free, widely-available digital games, as well as the affordances offered by digital technology has drawn new attention to the place of games in the language classroom (and outside). Christina Markanastasakis's study of a gamified approach in teaching vocabulary for English for academic purposes describes the pedagogical rationale behind the game's design and notes that it aims to raise motivation and foster an enjoyable learning experience. Bart Pardoel and his co-authors reflect on student use of a mobile game that they developed for learning German, which asks learners to become secret agents on a digital mission around Germany. Their findings reflect a positive response to the game from most learners. Jessica Zipf discusses her current project to develop a language learning game for Italian. She reflects on how lexical functional grammar architecture and components can benefit computer-assisted language learning within a grammar-based tool. She sees gamified elements as key future directions for the project, enhancing the learning experience.

Open education practice, the development of open content and Massive Open Online Courses (MOOCs) have been features of elearning symposia for some years. The papers in this volume give a snapshot of current research in these areas. Anna Comas-Quinn discusses her investigation into how language learning can be fostered through engagement with open, volunteer translation communities. She notes that the benefits outweigh the challenges and that the mix of informal and formal learning through distributed networks is a valuable model. The work discussed by Marina Orsini-Jones and Abraham Cerveró-Carrascosa features open content in combination with formal education. They explore trainee teacher beliefs about autonomy and online learning through the embedding of a MOOC in a classroom-based course of study. Their findings shed light on the value of repurposing MOOCs in this way. Rana Shahini and her co-authors take a closer look at MOOCs from a cultural perspective. They present a review of literature related to how aspects of multiculturalism are reflected in MOOCs and make recommendations for MOOC design.

We include two studies on telecollaboration projects. Intercultural, bilingual exchange facilitated by technology is popular amongst language students and teachers. Marta Fondo and Pedro Jacobetty describe a comparative study of two such telecollaborative projects undertaken with different groups of students. Their findings reveal the importance of project and task design. This recommendation is reflected by Lucy Watson's study of a telecollaborative project with international Foundation Year students. She highlights the cultural challenges that her project revealed and how planning, design, and flexibility are essential for the success of such projects.

Finally, we include two innovative approaches to familiar educational situations: field trips and orientation around a Virtual Learning Environment (VLE). Sarah Fielding shares her insights into using 360 image capture to create a mixed reality environment. She notes how easy to do this has become with recent software developments and makes recommendations for use of this technology in language teaching. Michael Salmon discusses his use of screencasts to guide international students around a VLE. He notes that this simple approach has great potential for enhancing the experience and understanding of international students (or any student) who is new to an institution's VLE.

We do hope you enjoy this volume of short papers from the eLearning Symposium and that you find inspiration and ideas for your own research and practice. We hope to see you at the symposium in the future, sharing your own work and experience.

1 Multilingual immersive communication technology: repurposing virtual reality for Italian teaching

Billy Brick[1], Tiziana Cervi-Wilson[2], Sean Graham[3], Tsvetan Tsankov[4], Michael Loizou[5], Nina Godson[6], and Kelly Ryan[7]

Abstract

This paper will report on a pilot Virtual Reality (VR) project which repurposes an existing scenario-based VR asset for health sciences. The original scenario aims to prepare health care students for home visits by allowing them to experience a semi-linear conversation with a virtual Non-Player Character (NPC). This provides a safe, non-threatening environment for students to hone the necessary skills they will need once they begin their professional careers. The NPC's simulated emotional state and reactions are changed based on the student's choice of responses. The original scenario was written in English but the opportunity to convert it into an Italian language learning resource by changing the audio files was identified and implemented. The scenario involves learners to be recurrently selecting from a number of possible responses in order to help the virtual character with his grievances regarding his father's care package.

1. Coventry University, Coventry, England; b.brick@coventry.ac.uk; https://orcid.org/0000-0002-2256-7046

2. Coventry University, Coventry, England; t.cervi@coventry.ac.uk; https://orcid.org/0000-0002-2754-5460

3. Coventry University, Coventry, England; hsx494@coventry.ac.uk; https://orcid.org/0000-0003-0635-7070

4. Coventry University, Coventry, England; ac1576@coventry.ac.uk

5. Coventry University, Coventry, England; ab8703@coventry.ac.uk; https://orcid.org/0000-0001-5603-7564

6. Coventry University, Coventry, England; hsx324@coventry.ac.uk

7. Coventry University, Coventry, England; aa7896@coventry.ac.uk

How to cite this chapter: Brick, B., Cervi-Wilson, T., Graham, S., Tsankov, T., Loizou. M., Godson, N., & Ryan, K. (2019). Multilingual immersive communication technology: repurposing virtual reality for Italian teaching. In A. Plutino, K. Borthwick & E. Corradini (Eds), *New educational landscapes: innovative perspectives in language learning and technology* (pp. 5-10). Research-publishing.net. https://doi.org/10.14705/rpnet.2019.36.949

Keywords: virtual reality, Italian, CEFR (B1), scenario-based learning, learning object, repurposing.

1.   Introduction

Although the notion of goggle-based VR can be traced back to the 1930s, it only began to be widely used in the form of Second Life from 2003 onwards. This platform boasted over 20 million members in 2010, but it is only fairly recently that VR has reached the mainstream, since the launch of several platforms in the sphere of gaming. The potential to incorporate VR technologies into language teaching was reported on widely by Godwin-Jones (2004), but still remains on the periphery in terms of methodologies due to their lack of sophistication and functionality compared to other commercial gaming products. However, the availability of cheaper stand-alone headsets has seen the emergence of numerous products designed specifically for language learning, including AltspaceVR, Mondly, ImmerseMe, VirtualSpeech, and Argotian (launches in 2019). In these safe spaces learners can practise their speaking skills and intercultural competencies. In spite of this, building suitable VR platforms remains expensive, especially in the higher education context where extensive funding for projects of this nature is difficult to secure in a subject area which is struggling to recruit students. Hence the idea to repurpose an already-existing health visitor VR asset, produced by colleagues in the Faculty of Health and Life Sciences, for language learning.

2.   Method

2.1.   The original asset

The original asset was built for health care students, using the Unity VR games development platform to practise home visits in a non-threatening environment. The asset enabled 30 undergrad health care students to interact for 15 minutes each with an NPC whose emotional state changed based on the students' responses. The state is updated and stored throughout the conversational process meaning that, at times, it could be more difficult to maintain a positive or neutral relationship with the NPC, giving the character a type of emotional memory. After the conversation has ended, the student is able to reflect on their choices through a replay system. During the replay, the student views their avatar through the eyes of the NPC whilst a coordinate system, which plots out the emotional state of the NPC, is shown alongside the avatar. This way the student can review and reflect on the choices they have made, and how it has had an emotional impact on the NPC. The choices are a combination of informative (activation) or uninformative (deactivation), and pleasant or unpleasant (see Figure 1). These choices, when made, apply a value to the emotional state of the NPC which is reflected on the following coordinate system.

Figure 1.   NPC emotional variance (Posner, Russell, & Peterson, 2005, n.p.)[8]

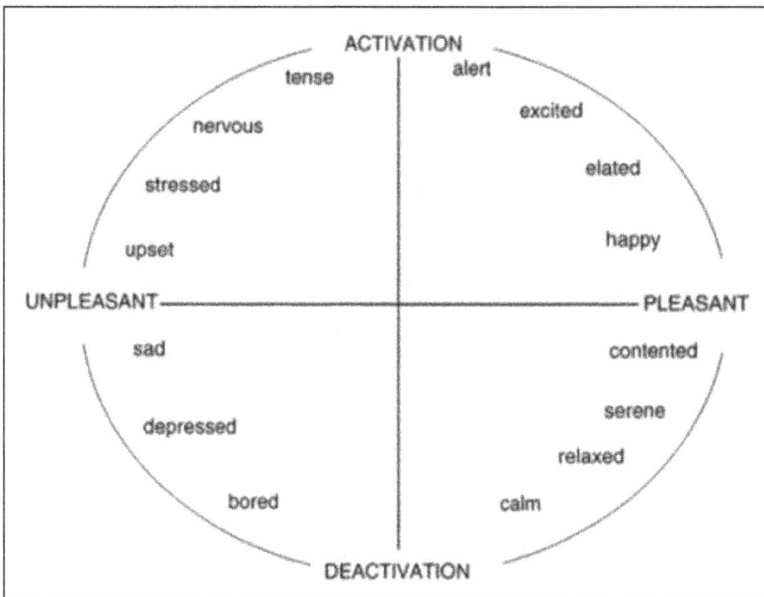

8. © 2005 Posner et al.; author manuscript before publication in final edited form

"Embodied learning is probably most effective when it is active, and the learner is not passively viewing the content, or watching others interact with manipulables" (Johnson-Glenberg, 2018, n.p.). By immersing the students in a virtual environment, some felt that it helped them to focus on the task.

2.2.   Repurposing the asset

Repurposing existing assets has been widespread in the humanities for some time, encouraged by the establishment of numerous repositories including the Humbox (Brick & Corradini, 2012) and LORO, the Open University's now-discontinued repository, in which academics deposited learning materials in written, audio, or visual formats to share with colleagues working in other institutions nationally and internationally. These materials could either be used in their entirety or repurposed providing the original author was acknowledged.

In the context of this project, this spirit of co-operation was expanded to work across subject areas and faculties. The aim of the project was to change the conversation between the NPC and the health care visitor from English to Italian and to do this, it was necessary to translate and replace the existing sound files from the original asset with Italian audio files. Three Italian (L1) speakers then voiced the dialogue which was professionally recorded before being uploaded in place of the English audio files to the VR asset. A further adjustment, using the dedicated software package Lipsync Pro, was needed in order to synchronise the characters with their new Italian responses.

3.   Results and discussion

The project is at a proof of concept stage only. However, the asset has the potential to allow learners to observe how the virtual character responds to their interactions, teaching them skills such as how to reason with an irate client, how to deal with complaints, and how to think and react in a foreign language in stressful situations. The finished asset could be employed in an Italian for specific purposes context or to help prepare students undertaking a year abroad.

Skills such as these are not explicitly taught on undergraduate programmes, therefore using VR technologies might offer affordances in this context. One of its innovative features is that student responses are sequentially plotted on a multi-polar coordinate system that records the virtual character's emotional state based on the participant's choices. The student can then reflect on their choices using a replay system that is viewed through the eyes of the virtual character (see Figure 2).

Figure 2.   Virtual character

The exercise can also be repeated as often as the student wants, which helps build confidence. Students could be encouraged to write down any new vocabulary they encounter during the session, providing contextualised learning opportunities in the field of learning languages for specific purposes. This would also teach students important employability skills and the asset could potentially be translated into any language, making it scalable in its application.

4.   Conclusions

Collaborating across disciplines within the university keeps the cost of VR development down and helps to forge communities of practice across faculties. The project proves that it is possible to repurpose VR assets into language learning resources by replacing the audio and written texts with other languages. Further collaborations are planned for testing the asset with colleagues from Southampton University. More work would be involved to change the body language and gestures associated with a particular culture as this would involve rerecording the motion capture.

Acknowledgements

We would like to thank Luca Morini and Pascal Carlucci for providing the Italian voices and the learning technologist Dan Wray for recording and editing the sound files essential for this project.

References

Brick, B., & Corradini, E. (2012). The HumBox: a teaching and learning repository for the humanities. In M. Orsini-Jones & L. Pibworth (Eds), *Language learning and teaching: Future Routes Conference Proceedings of the Joint Conference of the VLEs' Languages User Group's Vi Annual Conference and the Routes into Languages West Midland Consortium Conference* (pp. 38-46). Coventry

Godwin-Jones, R. (2004). Language in action: from webquests to virtual realities. *Language Learning & Technology, 8*(3), 9-14. https://doi.org/10125/25246

Johnson-Glenberg, M. C. (2018). Immersive VR and education: embodied design principles that include gesture and hand controls. *Frontiers in Robotics and AI.* https://doi.org/10.3389/frobt.2018.00081

Posner, J., Russell, J. A., & Peterson, B. S. (2005). *The circumplex model of affect: an integrative approach to affective neuroscience, cognitive development, and psychopathology* [Author manuscript]. https://www.ncbi.nlm.nih.gov/pmc/articles/PMC2367156/

2 A study on technology-based speech assistants

Serpil Meri-Yilan[1]

Abstract

This research aimed to look at students' perspectives on learning language through two technology-based speech recognition programmes, ImmerseMe and ELSA (English Language Speech Assistant). Data were collected from qualitative research instruments in April 2018. Five university-level students performed activities to improve their English and other languages in ImmerseMe for 30 minutes twice in two weeks, whereas they did activities to build up their English in ELSA once. The researcher observed them, and then interviewed them asking questions about their learning via these programmes. The findings showed that students had contrasting views on the programmes drawing attention to the programmes' benefits and potential improvements. This study demonstrated that Speech Recognition Technology (SRT) improved their speaking and listening skills. It makes recommendations for students, teachers, institutions, and designers to consider the effectiveness of SRT in language learning environments. It indicates the need to design a learning environment with a well-equipped programme.

Keywords: technology-based language learning, speech recognition system, ImmerseMe, ELSA.

1. Agri Ibrahim Cecen University, Agri, Turkey; serpilmeri@gmail.com; https://orcid.org/0000-0003-1132-568X

How to cite this chapter: Meri-Yilan, S. (2019). A study on technology-based speech assistants. In A. Plutino, K. Borthwick & E. Corradini (Eds), *New educational landscapes: innovative perspectives in language learning and technology* (pp. 11-17). Research-publishing.net. https://doi.org/10.14705/rpnet.2019.36.950

1.   Introduction

The advance in technology-based speech assistants has drawn attention to the use of commercial products, such as "Apple's Siri, Amazon's Alexa, Microsoft's Cortana, and Google's Assistant" (Hoy, 2018, p. 81), to complete tasks automatically (Johnson, 2013). These technology-based speech assistants help users through Automatic Speech Recognition (ASR) systems such as Speech-To-Text (STT), or Text-To-Speech (TTS) (Liakin, Cardoso, & Liakina, 2017).

Research in English as a foreign language has indicated the concerns of Non-Native Speakers (NNSs) to speak and listen to Native Speakers (NSs) of English (Shadiev, Hwang, Huang, & Liu, 2016). Although it is debatable whether ASR gives a "sufficiently correct" utterance or feedback (Rodman, 1999, p. 273), ASR helps NNSs first be understandable and have native-like speech in a long term (Bajorek, 2017). Recent studies have shown:

- NNSs' interaction with ASR and immediate feedback enhances speaking skills and positive views (Ahn & Lee, 2016);

- STT guides NNSs to apply different languages strategies (Shadiev et al., 2016);

- feedback, especially from ASR, is beneficial in improving pronunciation (Liakin et al., 2015, 2017);

- feedback provided by software is not enough for L2 pronunciation development (Bajorek, 2017);

- ELSA and Google Docs Voice Typing are a good opportunity for learners to hear their voice and correct their pronunciation (Bajorek, 2018a); and

- SRT embedded into lessons in ImmerseMe comforts speaking anxiety as NNSs practise language with NSs (Bajorek, 2018b).

Although these studies have suggested the implementation and design of learning programmes with ASR, there is still a research gap in how technology-based speech assistants support NNSs' speaking and listening skills. Considering the research gap in SRT, this study aimed to explore NNSs' perceptions of learning and developing to speak through embedded SRT programmes such as ImmerseMe and ELSA.

2. Method

2.1. Participants

This study involved five Turkish participants, three females and two males, aged between 19 and 22, studying in the preparatory class in the Department of Interpretation and Translation at Agri Ibrahim Cecen University, Turkey. Their English level was intermediate. All of them were unfamiliar with SRT systems embedded in learning programmes.

2.2. Speech recognition language learning programmes

This study applied two programmes, ImmerseMe and ELSA. ImmerseMe is a virtual reality-based language learning programme which has over 500 scenarios in nine different languages and makes a user speak in the dialogue perfectly to progress further in scenarios, which is feedback (ImmerseMe, 2018). In ImmerseMe, users travel through a 3D environment using the target language. However, ELSA is a technology-based speech assistant which focusses on and gives assessment and feedback on users' pronunciation and intonation (ELSA, 2018). When they succeed in speaking, the programme writes 'excellent'. In the contrary case, it provides feedback on the errors they make by giving suggestions on what to consider and examples of similar sounds of different words and showing their speech and the correct sound in the phonemic transcription and audio form. This study drew on the two programmes' features and their potential effects on speaking skills to explore students' perspectives of learning and improving speaking via these programmes.

2.3.   Data collection and analysis

Data were gathered from observations and follow-up semi-structured interviews in April 2018. During the observations, each participant performed English activities and one of the other languages for 30 minutes in ImmerseMe twice in two weeks, whereas each of them did English activities for ten minutes in ELSA once. The researcher did not interrupt them but observed their performance. After observation, they were interviewed to validate observation data (Charters, 2003) by responding to the question of how they thought about their learning.

Data sets were analysed in NVivo, coding the transcripts of participants' performances and perceptions of their learning in each programme according to the following categories: benefits, drawbacks, similarities, and differences.

3.   Results and discussion

Data from observations and interviews demonstrated that participants had positive views on SRT in ImmerseMe and ELSA. They believed that these programmes improved their speaking, as consistent with the studies by Bajorek (2018a, 2018b). However, this study compared the benefits and drawbacks of SRT provided by these programmes from the perspective of participants (see Table 1).

Table 1 shows that there is still a need to improve the programmes for the enhancement of speaking and listening skills. Along with the effect of these programmes on listening and speaking skills, participants thought that SRT in both programmes increased motivation and confidence.

This study showed that the more they used ImmerseMe, the more they felt comfortable in speaking and had fun with the activities and focussed on not only improving speaking skills but also travelling in an immersive 3D environment. However, in ELSA, they just focussed on their pronunciation and correct use of stress.

Table 1.   Benefits and drawbacks of ImmerseMe and ELSA stated in this study

	ImmerseMe	ELSA
Benefits	• Pronunciation improvement • Communication and interaction with NSs in a country where language is spoken in a 3D environment • Listening and speaking practice • Activities in different languages • Immediate feedback • Learning strategies development • Repeating NSs' speech • 360 degree videos	• STT system • Immediate written feedback on their speech and individual sounds • Listening and speaking practice • Pronunciation dictionary • Words in an example sentence and the international phonetic alphabet • Assessment (NS pronunciation score, needed work, proficiency level, conversation score) • Multiple activities • Seven day free trial
Drawbacks	• Just desktop-based programme • Weakness in recognising voices (i.e. soft voice, or a change because of sickness) • No phonetic and phonemic transcription of words • No STT system • The need for more scaffolding and feedback • No dictionary • Just British accent • No free trial activities	• Just mobile-based programme • Just American accent • No videos • No feedback about the assessment scores

4.   Conclusions

This study concludes that SRT provides NNSs with listening, speaking, and pronunciation development. SRT increases NNSs' motivation and confidence.

The study suggests that language learning programmes with SRT should be designed with adequate scaffolding and feedback, STT and TTS technology, free and easy use, and phonetic and phonemic transcriptions of sounds. Learning programmes should be considered with different accents and multiple activities with different languages. This study recommends NNSs to empower their pronunciation with learning programmes; teachers to bring programmes into learning environments; institutions to adapt technology-based learning environments into their classrooms; and designers to reconsider the suggested benefits and drawbacks of creating an ideal learning programme.

Acknowledgements

I would like to thank ImmerseMe for allowing me to conduct this research.

References

Ahn, T. Y., & Lee, S. M. (2016). User experience of a mobile speaking application with automatic speech recognition for EFL learning. *British Journal of Educational Technology*, *47*(4), 778-786. https://doi.org/10.1111/bjet.12354

Bajorek, J. P. (2017). L2 Pronunciation tools: the unrealized potential of prominent computer-assisted language learning software. *Issues and Trends in Educational Technology, 5*(2), 60-87.

Bajorek, J. P. (2018a). Speech technology for language learning: research & today's tools. *OLLReN*. http://ollren.org/ld.php?content_id=44618256

Bajorek, J. P. (2018b). *L2 virtual reality-based software, ImmerseMe: speaking, interactivity, and time*. Presented at Computer Assisted Lang. Instruction Consortium (CALICO), University of Illinois, Urbana-Champaign. https://www.academia.edu/36768999/Virtual_Reality_Technology_ImmerseMe_Software_Speaking_Interactivity_and_Time._Bajorek_2018_CALICO_2018

Charters, E. (2003). The use of think-aloud methods in qualitative research an introduction to think-aloud methods. *Brock Education Journal, 12*(2). https://doi.org/10.26522/brocked.v12i2.38

ELSA. (2018). *ELSA-Speak English fluently, easily, confidently.* https://www.elsaspeak.com/home

Hoy, M. B. (2018). Alexa, Siri, Cortana, and more: an introduction to voice assistants. *Medical reference services quarterly, 37*(1), 81-88. https://doi.org/10.1080/02763869.2018.1404391

ImmerseMe. (2018). *ImmerseMe: VR-based language learning.* https://immerseme.co/#home.

Johnson, S. A. P. (2013, June 14th). Language-learning software review: Babbel and Duolingo. *The Economist.* http://www.economist.com/blogs/johnson/2013/06/language-learning-software

Liakin, D., Cardoso, W., & Liakina, N. (2015). Learning L2 pronunciation with a mobile speech recognizer: French /y/. *CALICO Journal, 32*(1), 1-25. https://doi.org/10.1558/cj.v32i1.25962

Liakin, D., Cardoso, W., & Liakina, N. (2017). The pedagogical use of mobile speech synthesis (TTS): focus on French liaison. *Computer Assisted Language Learning, 30*(3-4), 325-342. https://doi.org/10.1080/09588221.2017.1312463

Rodman, R. (1999). *Computer speech technology.* Artech House.

Shadiev, R., Hwang, W. Y., Huang, Y. M., & Liu, C. J. (2016). Investigating applications of speech-to-text recognition technology for a face-to-face seminar to assist learning of non-native English-speaking participants. *Technology, Pedagogy and Education, 25*(1), 119-134. https://doi.org/10.1080/1475939X.2014.988744

3 Vocabulary Kingdom: gamified EAP vocabulary acquisition using blended learning

Christina Markanastasakis[1]

Abstract

Students in higher education should work on acquiring academic vocabulary as this is essential to skilfully communicating with other members of the academic community. Vocabulary acquisition is an essential but frequently neglected process due to the intensity, time pressure, and high stakes of short, assessment-based English for Academic Purposes (EAP) courses designed to prepare students for their postgraduate academic programme. Thus, in this experiment, student motivation to engage with vocabulary acquisition is considered in the context of Self-Determination Theory (SDT), which provides a framework for intrinsic and extrinsic motivation. In particular, intrinsic motivation is engendered by feelings of competence, autonomy, and relatedness; extrinsic motivation is rooted in quantifiable outcomes. With these theories in mind, Vocabulary Kingdom is a game that was created for an EAP, higher education classroom context, with the rationale of motivating students to spend more time engaged in vocabulary acquisition. This game features blended learning, with activities occurring in the classroom context and online.

Keywords: EAP, vocabulary acquisition, blended learning, gamification, motivation, self-determination theory.

1. University of Nottingham, Nottingham, England; cjmark.email@gmail.com

How to cite this chapter: Markanastasakis, C. (2019). Vocabulary Kingdom: gamified EAP vocabulary acquisition using blended learning. In A. Plutino, K. Borthwick & E. Corradini (Eds), *New educational landscapes: innovative perspectives in language learning and technology* (pp. 19-24). Research-publishing.net. https://doi.org/10.14705/rpnet.2019.36.951

1.   Introduction

Vocabulary Kingdom is a game that was conceived and designed by the author of this paper, who is a tutor of EAP. The purpose of this game is to support non-native speakers in a higher education context to acquire academic vocabulary, particularly during a foundation year course or a 12-week, pre-sessional, EAP course. In such intensive, assessment-based programmes, students may struggle to prioritise studying vocabulary despite its pervasive impact on their academic success. Moreover, studies have suggested that new vocabulary should be acquired incrementally on a daily basis; review and consolidation should occur continuously and consistently (Nagy & Townsend, 2012). Therefore, the intention is that Vocabulary Kingdom is motivational and specific to the course (Dörnyei & Csizér, 1998). Motivation engendered by the game is framed by the principles of SDT. The relevant framework relates to students' intrinsic motivation, elicited through feelings of autonomy, competence, and relatedness, as well as the extrinsic motivation of winning points for one's team.

2.   Method

2.1.   Game description

Students are divided into small groups consisting of three or four students; each group represents a tribe. Creating groups in the class is intended to foster a feeling of positive relatedness, which contributes to students' intrinsic motivation (Lombardi, in press). Group members decide on a tribe name and a group avatar.

Padlet was chosen as the suitable game platform for several reasons. First, it is user-friendly and easily accessed, as students can download and use the application on their mobile phone. Second, Padlet allows for the creation of a shared digital artefact which can be accessed and modified by several individuals simultaneously. Finally, Padlet was the most familiar platform to the tutor; according to Egenfeldt-Nielsen (2007), it is important that the facilitator is comfortable with the technology.

2.2.   Game objective

Students endeavour to acquire as many points as possible for their tribe in order to win the game and become the rulers of the Vocabulary Kingdom. This is achieved through daily and weekly activities, which are designed to support the vocabulary acquisition process. The points system is intended to augment students' extrinsic motivation to participate.

2.3.   Game rules

At the beginning of the game, the teacher ensures that students have access to the relevant academic word list. In addition, students may draw new vocabulary from class material.

Each student in the class, acting on behalf of their tribe, must enter a specified number of new academic words onto the Padlet each week. In addition to the word, each entry must include at least two of the following: other parts of speech, an example sentence, a synonym, and/or a relevant collocation.

2.4.   How the game is played

2.4.1.   Awarding points

The points system is ascertained by the tutor, in terms of how many points students will earn for their weekly entries of new words onto the Padlet; this system is shared with the students.

2.4.2.   Punitive measures

Punitive measures may be included in the game in order to impel participation and add intrigue to the game. In the pilot version, points were deducted for failure to participate by any tribe member, or if only one person did all the work. Creating punitive measures for non-participation ensures that complacency is kept to a minimum. Participation can be monitored through Padlet by the tutor/administrator.

2.4.3. Weekly challenge

The weekly challenge involves a competition during which students are shown pictures associated with the academic words on the Padlet; the tribe that gives the correct answer wins points, as predetermined by the teacher. Points may be deducted for incorrect answers, in order to deter students from randomly guessing. The method of using an image has been chosen because images are more likely to encapsulate the "abstract, technical, and nuanced ideas and phenomena" that are conveyed by academic vocabulary (Nagy & Townsend, 2012, p. 92). Associating an academic word with an image may enhance students' ability to recall it in another context, for example while reading a text.

At the end, the points are tallied up and the winner is determined. The tutor may ascertain a prize. During the pilot version, the other tribes were obligated to entertain the winning tribe at the farewell class party, by singing, dancing, or telling a story in English. Points are consequently associated with extrinsic rewards and become a motivating factor (Werbach & Hunter, 2012).

3.   Results and discussion

Player attachment to outcome is an essential feature and has an element of both intrinsic and extrinsic motivation, according to SDT (Juul, 2011; for SDT see Ryan, Rigby, & Przybylski, 2006). Moreover, the design of the game creates the conditions and contextual factors that enhance a sense of autonomy and competence, consequently augmenting the feeling of intrinsic motivation, an essential aspect of cognitive evaluation theory, a sub-theory of SDT (Ryan et al., 2006).

Several factors related to the points system contribute to students' extrinsic motivations to participate in the game. First, points serve as feedback and support students in assessing their own progress in learning new vocabulary (Werbach & Hunter, 2015). Students also feel motivated to create positive self-images in relation to classmates. Second, the points system provides each tribe with a variable, quantifiable outcome of gain or loss, which is an essential feature of game design (Juul, 2011). This means that students feel motivated to win points for their tribe and advance its progress within Vocabulary Kingdom. Furthermore, the points system enables tribes lagging behind to get ahead unexpectedly, which is a variable outcome that provides an element of surprise and further stimulates students' motivations (Dörnyei & Csizér, 1998; Werbach & Hunter, 2012). Finally, extrinsic motivation is created by the possibility of winning the game overall. In the pilot version, obligating classmates to provide entertainment at the final party proved to be an effective motivating factor.

The intrinsic motivation is derived from the feeling of competence and autonomy in making entries on the Padlet and the understanding that one's contribution has improved the tribe's overall performance. In addition, the relatedness of working together motivates students to contribute, not only for their own benefit, but for their group (Lombardi, in press). Moreover, students may begin to feel more competent on an academic level; they undoubtedly benefit from this acquired knowledge, as having a more expansive vocabulary will help them perform better academically (Nagy & Townsend, 2012).

The author observed that several academic words from Vocabulary Kingdom repeatedly appeared in several students' output during summative assessments, particularly writing tasks that were performed under time pressure. This suggests that Vocabulary Kingdom enhanced students' ability to actively draw on newly-acquired academic vocabulary. However, more research is needed and participant interviews may provide a greater insight into the process.

4. Conclusions

The purpose of Vocabulary Kingdom is to motivate students to engage with the process of acquiring academic vocabulary, an often neglected aspect of learning. The game is designed to ensure that students have a structured weekly format for learning vocabulary, a kind of 'check-point' every week, where they are reminded of their progress. The points system provides the feeling of extrinsic reward throughout the game. Intrinsic motivation is elicited through working individually and in tribes, which provides a feeling of competence, autonomy, and relatedness. In conclusion, this game is intended to motivate students to engage in an aspect of learning that is usually arduous, and to help them enjoy the process.

Acknowledgements

I would like to thank the members of class A57 of the University of Southampton Pre-Sessional 2018.

References

Dörnyei, Z., & Csizér, K. (1998). Ten commandments for motivating language learners: results of an empirical study. *Language teaching research*, *2*(3), 203-229.

Egenfeldt-Nielsen, S. (2007). *Educational potential of computer games*. Continuum.

Juul, J. (2011). *Half-real: video games between real rules and fictional worlds*. MIT Press.

Lombardi, I. (in press). *What video games can teach us about language learners' motivation*. https://www.academia.edu/5260967/What_Video_Games_Can_Teach_Us_About_Language_Learners_Motivation

Nagy, W., & Townsend, D. (2012). Words as tools: learning academic vocabulary as language acquisition. *Reading Research Quarterly*, *47*(1), 91-108. https://doi.org/10.1002/rrq.011

Ryan, R. M., Rigby, C. S., & Przybylski, A. (2006). The motivational pull of video games: a self-determination theory approach. *Motivation and emotion*, *30*(4), 344-360. https://doi.org/10.1007/s11031-006-9051-8

Werbach, K., & Hunter, D. (2012). *For the win: how game thinking can revolutionize your business*. Wharton Digital Press.

Werbach, K., & Hunter, D. (2015). *The gamification toolkit: dynamics, mechanics, and components for the win*. Wharton Digital Press.

4 MISSION BERLIN – a mobile gamified exploration of a new educational landscape

Bart Pardoel[1], Salomi Papadima-Sophocleous[2], and Androulla Athanasiou[3]

Abstract

Although the use of games and game elements other than pure entertainment has been studied in several academic fields, studies on completely gamified courses for foreign language learning in secondary schools are still scarce. This exploratory research paper contributes to a better understanding of the affordances of mobile gamification in Foreign Language (FL)/L2 education, specifically in the context of a Dutch secondary school. A technology-assisted mobile gamified language course for A1 German as an FL (GFL), called MISSION BERLIN, was developed, implemented, and evaluated. The students assumed the role of secret agents on a six-week mission to Germany's capital, using the official Moodle app on their own devices. A total number of 45,003 student's interactions (clicks) with the Moodle software were recorded and analysed, including the total number of individual interactions and the times when the clicks were made. In addition, the way how students collected the coins was analysed, making it possible to identify students' playing patterns and to explore different student actions.

Keywords: foreign language learning, gamification, Moodle, MALL.

1. Cyprus University of Technology, Limassol, Cyprus; b.pardoel@gmail.com; https://orcid.org/0000-0002-2667-0630

2. Cyprus University of Technology, Limassol, Cyprus; salomi.papadima@cut.ac.cy; https://orcid.org/0000-0003-4444-4482

3. Cyprus University of Technology, Limassol, Cyprus; androulla.athanasiou@cut.ac.cy

How to cite this chapter: Pardoel, B., Papadima-Sophocleous, S., & Athanasiou, A. (2019). MISSION BERLIN – a mobile gamified exploration of a new educational landscape. In A. Plutino, K. Borthwick & E. Corradini (Eds), *New educational landscapes: innovative perspectives in language learning and technology* (pp. 25-31). Research-publishing.net. https://doi.org/10.14705/rpnet.2019.36.952

1. Introduction

For the current generation of students, the use of digital and mobile technologies is considered a part of their daily lives. These 'digital natives' (Prensky, 2001) are used to a world in which action is triggered by rewards, fun, and competition (Zarzycka-Piskorz, 2016). Such elements are called *game elements* and they can be adapted for the needs arising during language classes (Danowska-Florczyk & Mostowski, 2014). In a well-balanced system, these game elements influence the players' actions, affect their considerations, and may change their behaviour over time. This fact is the basis of this study. The "process of making activities in non-game contexts more game-like by using game design elements" (Sailer, Hense, Mayr, & Mandl, 2017, p. 372) is a process called *gamification*, which draws from Ryan and Deci's (2000) *self-determination theory* and Csikszentmihályi's (1975) *theory of flow* .

In an earlier paper on this topic (Pardoel, Papadima-Sophocleous, & Athanasiou, 2018), we already explored the merits of the Moodle online platform for gamification and compared it to the Moodle app. This paper approaches the A1 GFL course from a user's perspective, in order to shed light on the players' interaction with the Moodle software. For this reason, an exploratory research was conducted, aiming to find out which playing patterns appear in a technology-assisted mobile gamified language programme at CEFR-A1 level. This course, called MISSION BERLIN, was then developed and implemented in Moodle.

2. Method

2.1. The setting

The study took place in a Dutch public pre-vocational school, a type of school with a relatively large number of students with special educational needs. The students (n=39, age=13/14) enrolled in the A1 GFL gamified course as an "intact class" (Mackey & Gass, 2005, p. 142). The students were familiar with playing (digital, board, or card) games. The course took six weeks; all students used their personal mobile devices and the school's Wifi connection.

2.2.   Research design and data collection

The student's interactions with the software, known as 'clicks', were automatically recorded in the Moodle logs. Examples of such clicks include the submission of work, completing group challenges, viewing documents, answering questions, or levelling up.

2.3.   The design of MISSION BERLIN

The students assumed the role of secret agents on a digital mission from Köln (Cologne) to Berlin by train, using the official Moodle app on their personal mobile devices. During this mission, they unlocked (or 'visited') the major cities of Germany by completing individual and collaborative challenges. The students had to complete a minimal amount of challenges to proceed to the next city, but were encouraged to complete as many activities per city as possible. To a certain degree, they were autonomous in their decision of which city to visit, however, the final destination, Berlin, always required 15 coins. Since the players gained only one or two coins per city, they needed to complete challenges in several cities to collect enough coins. With the exception of the starting city, each new city was only unlocked if two conditions simultaneously were true: (1) the player possessed the correct train ticket; and (2) the minimum amount of coins was collected. Coins could only be collected after successfully completing *group* challenges.

As shown in Figure 1, this design forced the players to visit core cities (e.g. Düsseldorf), but also encouraged them to visit side-track cities, such as Stuttgart. The same semi-autonomous structure also applies within the cities, where some activities were necessary to proceed and others were optional. An extended description of MISSION BERLIN can be found in Pardoel (2018).

Figure 1.   Amount of coins needed to unlock/access the next city

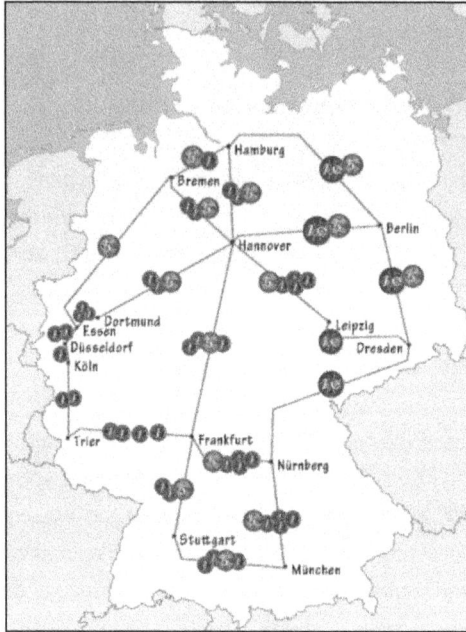

3.   Results and discussion

In total, 45,003 clicks were automatically recorded by Moodle, meaning that each student on average interacted 1,154 times ($\sigma=282$) with the software. After analysing the clicks in the Moodle logs, we could identify different kinds of players. Six students (clicks between 576 and 776) were considered to have a Low Activity (LA), seven students (clicks between 1,427 and 1,771) were labelled as High Activity (HA). As MISSION BERLIN was a school-only activity, it was expected to see clicks during school hours only. This was not the case: 9,790 clicks were recorded outside school hours. Except for one student, every other student opened the programme in their free time. However, there was a difference between the LA and HA group: on average 45% of the HA clicks were recorded outside school hours, for LA students this was only 5%.

Figure 2.   The four playing patterns, adapted from Pardoel (2018, p. 70)

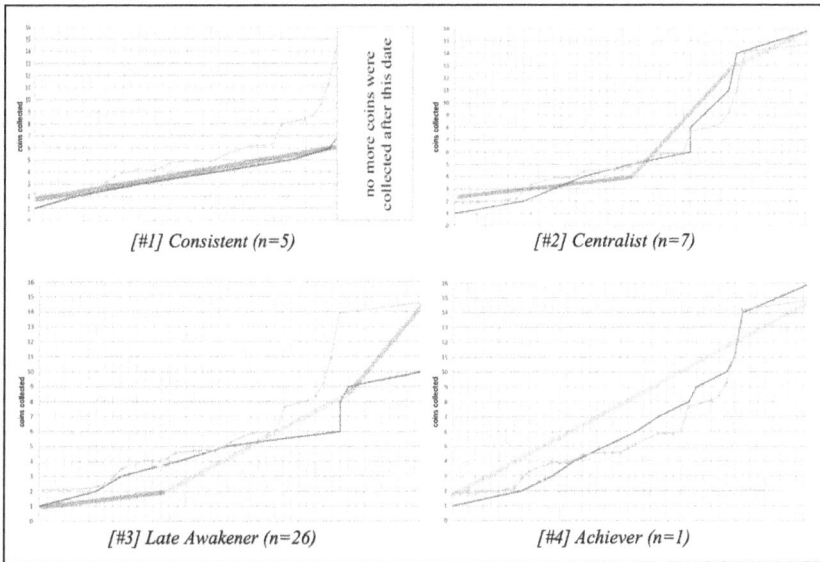

[#1] Consistent (n=5)

[#2] Centralist (n=7)

[#3] Late Awakener (n=26)

[#4] Achiever (n=1)

A reward schedule is the timeframe and delivery mechanism through which rewards are delivered (Raymer, 2011). Rewards are essentially a way to measure the student's achievements. The individual amount of coins, compared with the average amount of coins in the game, is an indication of the students' relative progress. Therefore, records showing an increase in number of coins collected enabled us to identify four different playing patterns: consistent, achiever, centralist, and late awakener (see Figure 2 above). Consistent players showed no increase or decrease in their coins collecting speed and tended to finish only the minimum of the required tasks to move. Achievers went beyond the minimal requirements and completed extra tasks. Centralist players started slowly, but after some time they increased their activity, only to fall back after the final objective of the game was reached. Similarly, late awakeners neglected the tasks at first, but once they noticed they were falling behind, they started participating. Our playing patterns show similarities to the four gamified leaderboard profiles as identified by Barata, Gama, Jorge, and Gonçalves (2013), however, MISSION BERLIN contains a considerably larger percentage of late awakeners.

4.   Conclusions

This paper explored playing patterns of players in a technology-assisted mobile gamified language programme at A1 level with the Moodle software, thus contributing to a better understanding of the affordances of mobile gamification in FL/L2 education.

Results indicate that HA students tend to interact with MISSION BERLIN in their free time almost as much as during school hours, unlike the LA students who seem to prefer playing mostly at school.

The study of the collaborative work in collecting coins highlighted four individual playing patterns.

The majority of the students were identified as late awakeners. Despite the fact that students were encouraged to collect more coins than necessary for their journey, only the achiever and centralist players have actively done so. The overall results indicate the need to further explore the difference in patterns between the two types of students as well as their interactions with the game.

References

Barata, G., Gama, S., Jorge, J., & Gonçalves, D. (2013). So fun it hurts - gamifying an engeneering course, *8027*(July), 639-648. https://doi.org/10.1007/978-3-642-39454-6

Csikszentmihályi, M. (1975). Beyond boredom and anxiety: experiencing flow in work and play. *The Jossey-Bass Behavioral Science Series*, 231.

Danowska-Florczyk, E., & Mostowski, P. (2014). Gamification as a new direction in teaching Polish as a foreign language. *ICT for Language Learning*. https://conference.pixel-online. net/conferences/ICT4LL2012/common/download/Paper_pdf/272-IBT55-FP-Florczyk-ICT2012.pdf

Mackey, A., & Gass, S. M. (2005). *Second language research: methodology and design* (2nd ed.). Lawrence Erlbaum Associates.

Pardoel, B. (2018). *Gamification and its potential for foreign language learning – lessons from a six-week gamified Moodle course for German as a foreign language at secondary school level.* Cyprus University of Technology. http://ktisis.cut.ac.cy/handle/10488/12944

Pardoel, B., Papadima-Sophocleous, S., & Athanasiou, A. (2018). How MISSION BERLIN gamified my FL / L2-German class – a six-week journey. In P. Taalas, J. Jalkanen, L. Bradley & S. Thouësny (Eds), *Future-proof CALL: language learning as exploration and encounters – short papers from EUROCALL 2018* (pp. 255-260). Research-publishing. net. https://doi.org/10.14705/rpnet.2018.26.846

Prensky, M. (2001). Digital natives, digital immigrants part 1. *On the Horizon, 9*(5), 1-6.

Raymer, R. (2011). Gamification: using game mechanics to enhance elearning. *eLearn magazine, 2011*(9). https://doi.org/10.1145/2025356.2031772

Ryan, R. M., & Deci, E. L. (2000). Self-determination theory and the facilitation of intrinsic motivation, social development, and well-being. *American Psychologist, 55*(1), 68-78. https://doi.org/10.1037//0003-066x.55.1.68

Sailer, M., Hense, J. U., Mayr, S. K., & Mandl, H. (2017). How gamification motivates: an experimental study of the effects of specific game design elements on psychological need satisfaction. *Computers in Human Behavior, 69*, 371-380. https://doi.org/10.1016/j.chb.2016.12.033

Zarzycka-Piskorz, E. (2016). Kahoot it or not? Can games be motivating in learning grammar? *Teaching English with Technology, 16*(3), 17-36.

5 A deep linguistic computer-assisted language learning game for Italian

Jessica Zipf[1]

Abstract

This paper describes the initial stages of a project which seeks to develop a language learning game for Italian running a deep linguistic grammar at its backend for fine-grained error detection. The grammar is designed within the grammatical framework of Lexical Functional Grammar (LFG). The project aims to bring together work from different fields by combining strategies from computational linguistics with theoretical insights from Second Language Acquisition (SLA) and components from computer gaming.

Keywords: Italian, SLA, lexical-functional grammar, gaming.

1. Introduction

In recent years, many tools have been developed to facilitate language learning. Aside from commercial products such as Duolingo (Teske, 2017) or HelloTalk (Rivera, 2017), grammar checkers based on linguistic frameworks have been implemented as well. These include a grammar checker for German (Fortmann & Forst, 2004) based on a large-scale LFG grammar, and *Arboretum* (Bender et al., 2004), a tutorial system for English using Flickinger's (2000) English Resource Grammar at its backend.

1. University of Konstanz, Konstanz, Germany; jessica.zipf@uni-konstanz.de; https://orcid.org/0000-0002-5264-0769

How to cite this chapter: Zipf, J. (2019). A deep linguistic computer-assisted language learning game for Italian. In A. Plutino, K. Borthwick & E. Corradini (Eds), *New educational landscapes: innovative perspectives in language learning and technology* (pp. 33-40). Research-publishing.net. https://doi.org/10.14705/rpnet.2019.36.953

© 2019 Jessica Zipf (CC BY)

While most commercially available systems rely on pattern-matching algorithms, grammar-based tools allow a more fine-grained error detection. Instead of comparing an input string to pre-programmed answers, a deep linguistic grammar analyses an input string morphologically and syntactically. The system developed here combines an LFG based grammar for Italian with a large-scale lexicon covering a wide range of Italian vocabulary. The grammar tool allows for the detection of errors and forms the building block for generating feedback to the learner. The actual learning process is guided by insights from processability theory (Bettoni & Di Biase, 2015; Pienemann, 2005), a theory of SLA that focusses on language development over time by analysing which forms from a second language are processable at which developmental stage (Pienemann, 2005). A recent publication discussing the development of Italian as a second language (Bettoni & Di Biase, 2015) is hereby fundamental for the exercise design and the order in which they are presented to the learners to ensure a successful language learning experience.

This paper aims to present the current state of the project by introducing the components that form the backbone of the computer-assisted language learning tool: the LFG based grammar and how its architecture and components are of great benefit.

2.   Method

Crucial to the tool is the combination of the following components: (1) concepts from Optimality Theory (OT) (Frank, King, Kuhn, & Maxwell, 1998) combined with error rules, (2) the generation component of the Xerox Linguistic Environment (XLE) (Crouch et al., 2008), and (3) the lexicon. Figure 1 illustrates the system's architecture and how these components feed into the language learning software.

The user interface is being fed by the LFG based grammar, alongside learning material. The grammar is responsible for evaluating free user input, generating feedback, and a corrected sentence or structure in case of erroneous input. The user is thus presented with an exercise, inputs their answer, and receives feedback. This information is then passed on to update the user data and subsequent tasks are adapted accordingly.

Figure 1. Architecture

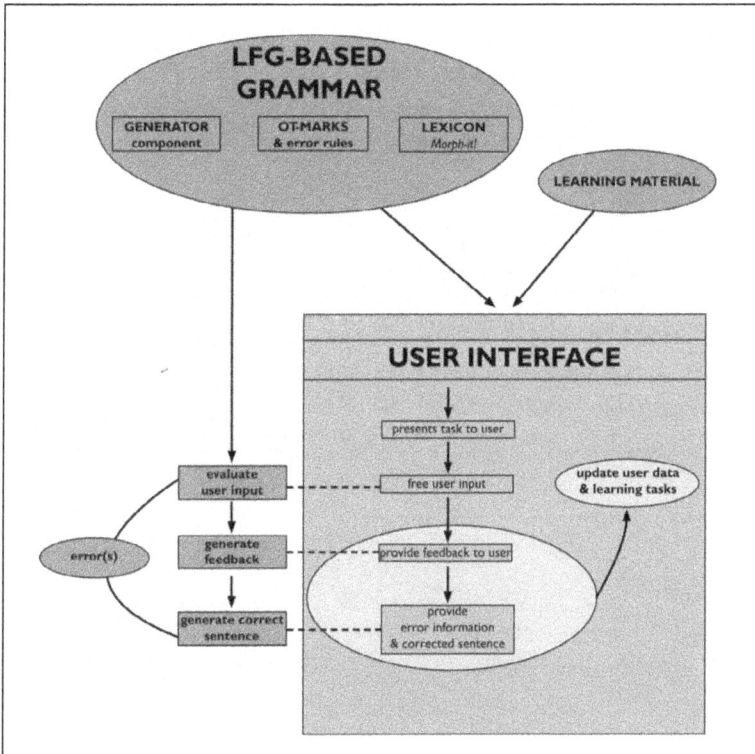

3. System components

3.1. Lexical Functional Grammar

LFG is a lexicalist, non-derivational theory of grammar (Dalrymple, 2001; Kaplan & Bresnan, 1982). In contrast to other generative grammars, LFG assumes parallel representations for sentences, each with its own structure and vocabulary, and adhering to its own constraints. Constituent structure and functional structure (c- and f-structure) are the two main representations for sentences. While a c-structure depicts hierarchical relations, constituency, and linearity in the shape of a syntactic tree, an f-structure captures grammatical functions and semantic notions such as tense and aspect in an attribute-value matrix. Having a strong mathematical architecture, LFG is not only implementable but also efficient and fast in analysing input. The Italian grammar in this project is implemented with XLE, a platform commonly used to implement LFG based grammars.

3.2.   OT marks

OT marks allow the statement of preferences and dis-preferences in sentence analysis and can be ordered according to their relative importance. As a result, these marks enable the system to deal with ambiguous and ungrammatical input. The mark *ungrammatical* is added to error rules in the grammar, allowing the parser to analyse ungrammatical sentences. Additionally, information on the error type can be added, passing this information on to an f-structure. Consider the subsequent sentence:

- Peter   mangi-o*   una   mela.
- Peter.**3PSG**   eat-**1PSG**   an   apple.
- 'Peter eats an apple'.

This is an example of erroneous subject-verb agreement. Parsing the sentence with the LFG grammar yields the following output (Figure 2).

While the c-structure on the left illustrates the constituents and the hierarchical structure, the f-structure contains semantic information on the main predicate and its arguments. Additionally, it returns the information that subject-verb agreement is ungrammatical in this example. This information is passed on to the f-structure by adding certain annotations to the OT mark *ungrammatical*.

Figure 2. C- and f-structure of Example 1

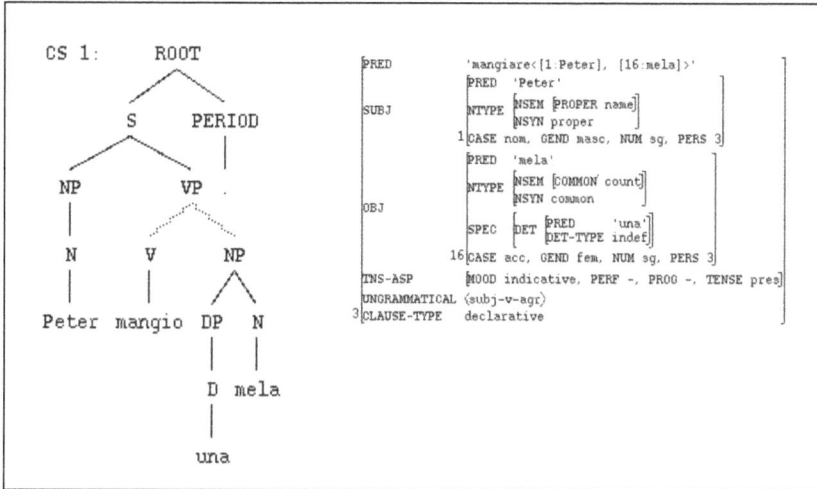

3.3. XLE generator

The generator component of XLE enables the system to create a sentence given an f-structure as input. Generation being the reverse of parsing, the same grammar produces a string based on a certain f-structure analysis. Here, the generator is used to provide a grammatical sentence given an ungrammatical input. Going back to Example 1, the XLE generator takes as input the f-structure in Figure 2 and produces the grammatical alternative depicted in Figure 3.

Figure 3. Grammatical alternative to Example 1 as generated by XLE

```
% parse "Peter mangio una mela."
parsing {Peter mangio una mela.}
1 solutions, 0.003 CPU seconds, 0.170MB max mem, 30 subtrees unified
1
%
Peter mangia una mela.
```

The first line illustrates the ungrammatical sentence that was passed on to the system, while the last line shows the grammatical alternative with subject-verb agreement satisfied.

3.4.　Lexicon

The lexicon constitutes the third big building block of the tool. It was created by converting the *Morph-it!* lexicon (Zanchetta & Baroni, 2005) into a finite state morphological analyser using the Xerox Finite State Tool (Beesley & Karttunen, 2003). The lexicon contains 34,968 lemmas and an overall count of 504,906 entries. Not only does it provide the grammar with a large Italian lexicon, but additionally with morphological analyses that expand from the c-structure, as depicted in Figure 4.

Figure 4.　Integrating a finite state morphological analyser

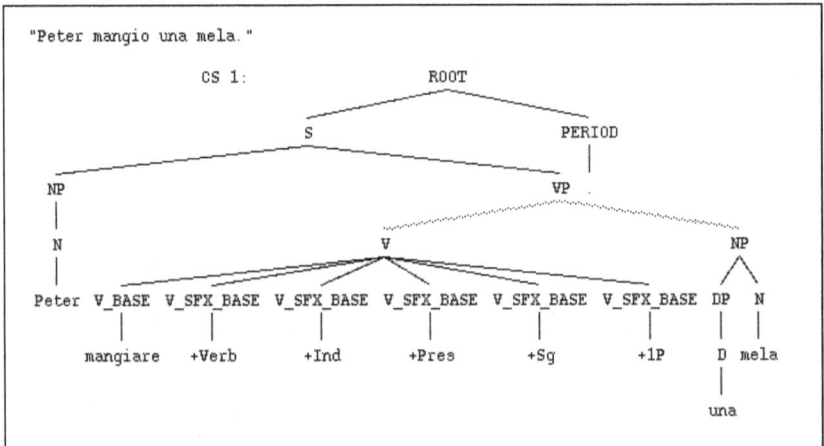

4.　Conclusions

This paper outlines an on-going project on the development of a language learning game for Italian. The tool is based on a deep grammar within the framework of LFG and integrates an Italian lexicon. While the grammar component is responsible for analysing the user input and returning adequate feedback, the learning process is to be guided by insights from the processability theory. At this initial stage of development, the grammar component can detect error types and return the grammatical alternatives. Next steps include further expansion of the grammar and its syntactic structures, an evaluation of the grammar using learner corpora, and the development of learning material and learning exercises. The final stages of the project are then to incorporate the grammar and the learning material into an attractive and user-friendly environment, including gaming components to enhance the learning experience.

Acknowledgements

I want to thank my supervisor Miriam Butt for the possibility to work on this project and her constant support and input, as well as Bruno Di Biase and Barbara Hinger for their input and discussions on SLA and processability theory.

References

Beesley, K. R., & Karttunen, L. (2003). *Finite state morphology*. CSLI Publications. http://www.fsmbook.com

Bender, E. M., Flickinger, D., Oepen, S., Walsh, A., & Baldwin, T. (2004). Arboretum: using a precision grammar for grammar checking in CALL. *Proceedings of the InSTILICALL2004 Symposium on ComputerAssisted Language Learning, 17*, 19. http://www.isca-speech.org/archive_open/archive_papers/icall2004/iic4_020.pdf

Bettoni, C., & Di Biase, B. (2015). The development of Italian as a second language. In C. Bettoni & B. Di Biase (Eds), *Grammatical development in second languages: exploring the boundaries of processability theory* (pp. 117-147). EuroSLA.

Crouch, D., Dalrymple, M., Kaplan, R. M., King, T. H., Maxwell, J., & Newman, P. (2008). XLE documentation. *Palo Alto Research Center*.

Dalrymple, M. (2001). *Lexical functional grammar*. Academic Press.

Flickinger, D. (2000). On building a more efficient grammar by exploiting types. *Natural Language Engineering, 6*(1), 15-28. https://doi.org/10.1017/S1351324900002370

Fortmann, C., & Forst, M. (2004). An LFG grammar checker for CALL. *Proceedings of InSTIL/ICALL2004 - NLP and Speech Technologies in Advanced Language Learning Systems*, (1), 2-5.

Frank, A., King, T., Kuhn, J., & Maxwell, J. (1998). Optimality theory style constraint ranking in large-scale LFG grammars. In *Proceedings of the LFG98 Conference*. Stanford: CSLI Publications. http://elib.uni-stuttgart.de/opus/volltexte/1999/356/

Kaplan, R. M., & Bresnan, J. (1982). Lexical-functional grammar: a formal system for grammatical representation. *Issues in Lexical-Functional Grammar, 8*(5), 29-130.

Pienemann, M. (Ed.). (2005). *Cross-linguistic aspects of processability theory*. John Benjamins.

Rivera, A. V. (2017). HelloTalk. *CALICO Journal, 34*(3), 384-392.

Teske, K. (2017). Duolingo. *CALICO Journal, 34*(3), 393-401.

Zanchetta, E., & Baroni, M. (2005). Morph-it! a free corpus-based morphological resource for the Italian language. *Corpus Linguistics 2005, 1*(1).

6 Using online volunteer translation communities for language learning in formal education

Anna Comas-Quinn[1]

Abstract

This paper reviews three attempts to incorporate technology-enabled online volunteer translation communities into language teaching in formal education. Through taking part in these communities, participants can develop many important skills, including digital, participatory, and information literacy, alongside improving their language skills and acquiring knowledge of translation and subtitling. Despite the challenges, an open pedagogy that connects learners with communities outside the classroom offers valuable opportunities to engage learners in meaningful tasks that add value to society, and relates well to a project-based, situated, and experiential pedagogy. Through an action research process, several activity designs for using TED Translators in language and translation education were implemented, evaluated, and refined to offer learners and teachers effective ways of engaging with this rich resource. An overview of the opportunities and challenges is presented, including ethical considerations of using open online communities in formal language education.

Keywords: translation education, language learning, open pedagogy, situated learning, TED Translators.

1. The Open University, Milton Keynes, England; anna.comas-quinn@open.ac.uk; https://orcid.org/0000-0002-8290-4315

How to cite this chapter: Comas-Quinn, A. (2019). Using online volunteer translation communities for language learning in formal education. In A. Plutino, K. Borthwick & E. Corradini (Eds), *New educational landscapes: innovative perspectives in language learning and technology* (pp. 41-46). Research-publishing.net. https://doi.org/10.14705/rpnet.2019.36.954

1. Introduction

Technology has made possible the creation of online communities in which participants engage in voluntary activities to produce and consume content. TED Translators is one example: over 30,000 volunteers transcribe, translate, and review the subtitles of TED Talks into over 100 languages. In the process, they develop a number of skills, both linguistic (vocabulary building, translation, writing…) and organisational and transversal, such as digital literacy, online collaboration, or research. Motivation to participate ranges from enjoyment of the activity and affinity with the mission of spreading knowledge across languages (Cámara de la Fuente, 2014) to an interest in developing translation and subtitling skills as part of a path towards professional translation.

There is great potential in the learning opportunities afforded by these communities as part of learner-directed informal learning but also in more formal educational contexts (Wikipedia Education Program, 2012). Besides the chance to engage students in a meaningful, real-world task that makes a visible contribution to society, working with these open communities fits well with an open pedagogy (Beetham, Falconer, McGill, & Littlejohn, 2012) based on project-based, situated, and experiential principles (González-Davies & Enríquez-Raído, 2016; Kiraly, 2016). This brief paper examines the potential of using these communities in formal educational contexts whilst acknowledging the challenges, as the rigid schedules of formal education rarely match the more relaxed and unpredictable rhythms of volunteer activities.

2. Ways of working with TED Translators

The learning designs trialled to engage higher education language and translation learners with TED Translators are briefly described here in chronological order, and further information can be obtained from the relevant publications.

In a first pilot project (Cámara de la Fuente & Comas-Quinn, 2016), five translation graduates from the Universidad de Valladolid, Spain, volunteered to take part in a teacher-guided activity that introduced them to TED Translators and to translating the subtitles of a talk. The teachers, who are TED Translator volunteers themselves, arranged for the tasks to be reviewed, approved, and published within the time scheduled for the activity. The number of participants was small and the feedback largely positive, but a number of challenges became evident: the steep learning curve to deal with the technical side of the task; the lack of familiarity or acceptance of community customs which led to most learners using the wrong form of address in their translations as they chose Peninsular Spanish over the Global Spanish convention agreed by the community; the impossibility of scaling up a design that relied on teacher input to overcome the delays in review and approval inherent in a volunteer project; and, in the case of one participant, the rejection of volunteering as a legitimate learning activity.

The second project (Comas-Quinn & Fuertes Gutiérrez, 2017) involved several language combinations and 15 students, all language graduates from The Open University, UK. The activity introduced them to translation and subtitling, and to ways of using online open and free content to keep up their language skills post-graduation. The activity design was expanded to include a peer review stage once the translation was completed so that participants could give and receive feedback to improve their work before deciding whether to submit it to the TED Translators review process for publication. Some technical challenges were experienced by participants but, with one exception, they all reported a very positive experience which included high levels of enjoyment and the discovery of a new recreational or professional interest. This project also trialled a way of assessing the activity through a reflective essay in which participants were asked to comment on linguistic, cultural, and technical challenges encountered in the task.

Other ways of using TED Translators in language learning have been incorporated into the Master of Arts in translation at The Open University, UK. In the section 'gaining experience', students are introduced to volunteering as a way of practising their translation skills, building up a portfolio of work to showcase to prospective employers, and networking with other professionals. When they study 'audiovisual translation', they are directed to TED Translators where they can practise their subtitling skills using an open-source subtitling editor (Amara). Beaven (forthcoming) explains how in their 'language development' work, students are directed to TED Talks to build up-to-date technical vocabulary in their chosen area of specialisation. Students are not required to volunteer for TED Translators and their participation is not assessed.

3.   Results and discussion

Sauro (2017) notes that support is not universal for "domesticating language-learning practices from the digital wilds to the formal classroom" (p. 140). Teachers attempting this should be mindful of preserving key components of learning in online communities, such as self-direction, collaboration, and engagement (Curwood, 2013), and of respecting the cultures of the communities the learners and teachers are entering (Minkel, 2015).

Ethical considerations need to be contemplated and managed too when directing learners to volunteer communities. Besides some negative perceptions of volunteering (Cámara de la Fuente & Comas-Quinn, 2016) shared by some translation scholars (O'Hagan, 2012), there is an ethical contradiction in mandating learners to volunteer or to create content to be published openly online (Martínez-Arboleda, 2014). Designs that allow learners to make these decisions themselves can be developed to allow different paths to participation and respect learners' ownership of their own time and content.

4.   Conclusions

Open pedagogy is a way of bringing formal and informal learning contexts together and placing knowledge production in the hands of learners in a more distributed knowledge and expertise model that builds on and better reflects the connected nature of our digital society. In the projects reported here, the teacher's role is to direct learners to existing learning opportunities, helping them to recognise and take advantage of these opportunities, whilst retaining their right to make their own decisions.

References

Beaven, T. (forthcoming). 'Your language development': harnessing openness to integrate independent language learning into the curriculum. In A. Comas-Quinn, A. Beaven & B. Sawhill (Eds), *New case studies of openness in and beyond the language classroom*. Research-publishing.net.

Beetham, H., Falconer, I., McGill, L., & Littlejohn, A. (2012). *JISC open practices: briefing paper*. https://oersynth.pbworks.com/w/page/51668352/OpenPracticesBriefing

Cámara de la Fuente, L. (2014). Multilingual crowdsourcing motivation on global social media, case study: TED OTP. *Sendebar, 25*, 197-218.

Cámara de la Fuente, L., & Comas-Quinn, A. (2016). Situated learning in open communities: the TED Open Translation project. In P. Blessinger & T. J. Bliss (Eds), *Open education: international perspectives in higher education*. Open Book Publishers. https://doi.org/10.11647/obp.0103.05

Comas-Quinn, A., & Fuertes Gutiérrez, M. (2017). 'An interest in translation and a great addition to the CV!' An evaluation of learners' experiences of an online volunteering task. OER17, London, 5–6 April 2017. http://oro.open.ac.uk/54898/

Curwood, J. S. (2013). Fan fiction, remix culture, and The Potter Games. In V .E. Frankel (Ed.), *Teaching with Harry Potter* (pp. 81-92). McFarland.

González-Davies, M., & Enríquez-Raído, V. (2016). Situated learning in translator and interpreter training: bridging research and good practice. *The Interpreter and Translator Trainer, 10*(1), 1-11. https://doi.org/10.1080/1750399x.2016.1154339

Kiraly, D. (Ed.). (2016). *Towards authentic experiential learning in translator education*. Mainz University Press.

Martínez-Arboleda, A. (2014). *The ethics of student digital publication*. OER14 Conference, University of Newcastle, 29 April 2014. https://oer14.oerconf.org/archive/14/oer14/92/view/index.html

Minkel, E. (2015, March 25). From the Internet to the Ivy League: fan fiction in the classroom. https://themillions.com/2015/03/from-the-internet-to-the-ivy-league-fanfiction-in-the-classroom.html

O'Hagan, M. (2012). From fan translation to crowdsourcing: consequences of Web 2.0 empowerment in audiovisual translation. In A. Ramael, P. Orero & M. Carroll (Eds), *Audiovisual translation and media accessibility at the crossroads* (pp. 25-41). Rodopi. https://doi.org/10.1163/9789401207812

Sauro, S. (2017). Online fan practices and CALL. *CALICO Journal, 34*(2), 131-46. https://doi.org/10.1558/cj.33077

Wikipedia Education Program. (2012). *Case studies: how professors are teaching with Wikipedia.* Wikimedia Foundation. http://upload.wikimedia.org/wikipedia/commons/0/03/Wikipedia_Education_Program_Case_Studies.pdf

7 BMELTET – Blending MOOCs into English language teacher education with telecollaboration

Marina Orsini-Jones[1] and Abraham Cerveró Carrascosa[2]

Abstract

This paper reports on how the FutureLearn Massive Open Online Course (MOOC) *Becoming a Better Teacher* was blended into English Language Teaching (ELT) university programmes in conjunction with telecollaboration. It discusses how the addition of a MOOC blend can enhance a telecollaborative exchange by adding to it increased opportunities for social collaborative interaction on a global scale. Blending MOOCs into English Teacher Education with Telecollaboration (BMELTET) fosters the students' reflection on online and blended learning and teaching to support their future teaching practice. The paper illustrates how participating students – undergraduate ELT students from Spain and postgraduate ELT students studying in the UK – participated in both synchronous and asynchronous exchanges on the MOOC content. The discussion will focus on how a holistic approach to the integration of technology into language teacher education programmes with a blend of formal and informal platforms can support students in reflecting on their beliefs.

Keywords: MOOCs, ELT, blended, telecollaboration.

1. Coventry University, Coventry, England; m.orsini@coventry.ac.uk; https://orcid.org/0000-0001-5250-5682

2. Florida Universitària, Valencia, Spain; acervero@florida-uni.es

How to cite this chapter: Orsini-Jones, M., & Cerveró Carrascosa, A. (2019). BMELTET – Blending MOOCs into English language teacher education with telecollaboration. In A. Plutino, K. Borthwick & E. Corradini (Eds), *New educational landscapes: innovative perspectives in language learning and technology* (pp. 47-53). Research-publishing.net. https://doi.org/10.14705/rpnet.2019.36.955

47

1.   Introduction

Telecollaboration can foster the development of Intercultural Communicative Competence (ICC) for the digital age (Helm & Guth, 2010, p. 74; Müller-Hartmann & O'Dowd, 2017, p. 2; Lloyd, Cerveró-Carrascosa, & Green, 2018; Orsini-Jones & Lee, 2018). It enables participants to develop both the intercultural 'savoirs' proposed by Byram, Gribkova, and Starkey (2002), and also their media literacy.

Previous related studies illustrated that embedding an existing MOOC that is relevant to the syllabus covered by students engaged in teacher education, and combining it with telecollaboration, appears to enhance participants' critical digital literacy and ICC (Orsini-Jones, Conde Gafaro, & Altamimi, 2017). Such projects can moreover help with dispelling existing negative beliefs about e-learning held by students engaged in ELT teacher education (Orsini-Jones et al., 2018).

BMELTET involved undergraduate ELT students from Florida Universitària (FU) in Spain and postgraduate ELT students studying at Coventry University (CU) in the UK. The integration of the FutureLearn MOOC *Becoming a Better Teacher: Enhancing Professional Development* (designed by the British Council and University College London, Institute of Education) into the existing curriculum in the two institutions offered the opportunity for students to reflect on their professional development with a worldwide community of practice. The main research question posed was whether or not BMELTET could support students in ELT education in adopting a holistic approach to the integration of technology in their future practice while developing their ICC.

2.   Method

2.1.   Participants

This study discusses the occurrence of the BMELTET project that was carried out between September and December 2017. The Spanish participants were 12 third year undergraduate students on a four-year degree course (Bachelor of Arts in primary education). They were all Spanish nationals, between 18-30 years of age. Fifty-six percent had prior teaching experience.

The students based in the UK were 26, from a variety of different nationalities: 15 Chinese, six British, and one respectively from Taiwan, Malaysia, South Korea, the Netherlands, and Pakistan; they were between 21-60 years of age. Fifty-four percent had prior teaching experience.

2.2.　Procedure

All participants read and signed a consent form that had been approved by the ethics governance unit at CU and agreed to:

- fill in a pre-project and post-project online survey;

- engage with the *Becoming a Better Teacher* MOOC for three hours per week for the four weeks of its duration, while also doing their related ELT course face-to-face and engaging in telecollaboration with their partners;

- record their reflections on how their learning experience was affected by the MOOC platform and its global social collaborative features while engaging with it in three ways: in the MOOC discussion, face-to-face in class, and on the dedicated Moodle telecollaborative discussion; and

- participate in two class-to-class live Skype reflective sessions.

2.3.　Tasks

A dedicated Moodle BMELTET website was created to enable participants to discuss specific units in the MOOC. A Skype all-class session was carried out for two of the tasks related to the MOOC topics and the relevant curricular content linked to the MOOC in each institutional programme. Students posted their reflections both in the discussions in Moodle and in the MOOC. Live Moodle Chat was also used, but proved to be less effective than asynchronous forum postings and Skype exchanges.

The first week focused, for example, on the conceptualisation of Continuous Professional Development (CPD) on the MOOC. Students were invited to take part in the MOOC discussion and reflect on this experience individually in the relevant Moodle forum. Subsequently, they were paired up (one from FU and one from CU) to post together on the topics covered on the MOOC in the Moodle forums. Another task involved working on 'valid and desirable principles' to apply to language learning and teaching (see Figure 1, a screen shot from the Moodle discussion that supported the project).

Figure 1.   Screen shot of telecollaborative pair reflection

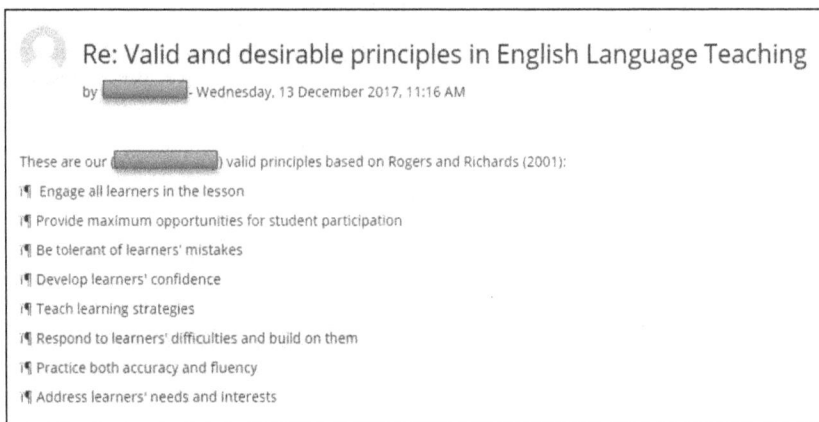

> Re: Valid and desirable principles in English Language Teaching
> by ▆▆▆▆▆ - Wednesday, 13 December 2017, 11:16 AM
>
> These are our (▆▆▆▆▆) valid principles based on Rogers and Richards (2001):
> ¶ Engage all learners in the lesson
> ¶ Provide maximum opportunities for student participation
> ¶ Be tolerant of learners' mistakes
> ¶ Develop learners' confidence
> ¶ Teach learning strategies
> ¶ Respond to learners' difficulties and build on them
> ¶ Practice both accuracy and fluency
> ¶ Address learners' needs and interests

3.   Results and discussion

In the pre-BMELTET survey, there was a marked difference between the participants from FU and CU regarding their initial awareness of what a MOOC is: only 46% of the participants from CU against 89% from FU. The fact that most CU participants were from overseas would appear to be a factor here.

Another difference in the pre-BMELTET survey had to do with the perception of usefulness of online learning. The statement set was: 'online learning is not suitable for language learning'. While 66.9% of FU participants chose either 'mostly disagree' or 'strongly disagree', with only 33.3% 'neither agree nor disagree', the breakdown for CU was a 57.7% of positive feedback and 42.3% negative.

None of the participants had taken part in telecollaboration before BMELTET.

The post-BMELTET survey highlighted a shift in position amongst CU participants, who appeared to align with FU participants in having found the experience of engaging online with a MOOC and with telecollaboration.

The major findings from the survey were:

- 70% of participants agreed that engaging with the BMELTET project changed their beliefs as a teacher;

- 80% agreed that the MOOC discussions made them feel part of a worldwide community of practice;

- 60% agreed that taking part in the project had changed their beliefs on online learning (in a positive way); and

- 80% agreed that the project had helped them with reflecting on their teaching practice in a novel way.

A small group of students (10%) did however write in the open comments that they still preferred a face-to-face mode of instruction to a blended or distance one, e.g. "Actually, even if we need to use technology, I'd prefer to be taught in traditional ways" (Student A).

A limitation of these findings is that the participation in the post-BMELTET survey was considerably lower (31% of all participants) than in the pre-

BMELTET one (85% of all participants). All students however commented positively on the telecollaborative Skype exchanges during oral feedback sessions, which had enabled them to discuss specific intercultural issues relating to their teaching contexts.

The encouraging results reported above are summarised well in this comment extracted from the post-BMELTET survey: "[It] is a good and interesting experience. I would put it into practice for the future because I am learning a lot" (Student B).

4.   Conclusions

All participants commented positively on how the project had made them aware of the potential of online and blended learning for ELT and made them realise that online collaboration, both via MOOCs and telecollaboration, was useful for the purpose of enhancing their CPD, their reflective practice and their ICC. Not all students were however at ease with the project and some found it challenging because of its digital complexities (number of digital platforms used and passwords to handle). Nevertheless, the data collected and discussed here demonstrate evidence of a shift in positive beliefs towards online and blended learning for most participants and an appreciation of the 'added value' of blended learning, which, it is hoped, will support a holistic approach to the adoption of technology in their future practice[3].

Acknowledgements

We would like to thank all the students who participated in this project between September and December 2017.

---

3. The authors are aware of the fact that the General Data Protection Regulation introduced in May 2018 might limit the opportunity to mix formal and informal learning discussed here.

References

Byram, M., Gribkova, B., & Starkey, H. (2002). *Developing the intercultural dimension in language teaching: a practical introduction for teachers*. Council of Europe.

Helm, F., & Guth S. (2010). The multifarious goals of telecollaboration 2.0: theoretical and practical implications. In S. Guth & F. Helm (Eds), *Telecollaboration 2.0* (pp 69-106). Peter Lang. https://doi.org/10.3726/978-3-0351-0013-6

Lloyd, E., Cerveró-Carrascosa, A., & Green, C. (2018). A role-reversal model of telecollaborative practice: the student-driven and student-managed FloCo. In M. Orsini-Jones & S. Smith (Eds), *Flipping the blend through MOOCs, MALL and OIL – new directions in CALL* (pp. 51-58). Research-publishing.net. https://doi.org/10.14705/rpnet.2018.23.790

Müller-Hartmann, A., O'Dowd, R. (2017). *A training manual on telecollaboration for teacher trainers.* https://www.evaluateproject.eu/evlt-data/uploads/2017/09/Training-Manual_EVALUATE.pdf

Orsini-Jones, M., Conde, B., Borthwick, K., Zou, B., & Ma, W. (2018). *BMELTT: blending MOOCs for English language teacher training*. Teaching English, ELT Research Papers 18.02, British Council. https://www.teachingenglish.org.uk/sites/teacheng/files/Pub_J121_Blending%20MOOCs%20for%20English%20language%20teacher%20training_FINAL_Web.pdf

Orsini-Jones, M., Conde Gafaro, B., & Altamimi, S. (2017). Integrating a MOOC into the Postgraduate ELT curriculum: reflecting on students' beliefs with a MOOC blend. In Q. Kan & S. Bax (Eds), *Beyond the language classroom: researching MOOCS and other innovations* (pp.1-13). Research-publishing.net. https://doi.org/10.14705/rpnet.2017.mooc2016.672

Orsini-Jones, M., & Lee, F. (2018). *Intercultural communicative competence for global citizenship: identifying rules of engagement in telecollaboration*. Palgrave MacMillan

8 Design recommendations to address cultural issues in multicultural MOOCs: a systematic literature review

Rana Shahini[1], Hugh C. Davis[2], and Kate Borthwick[3]

Abstract

One of the goals of Massive Open Online Courses (MOOCs) is to democratise education. With their unique openness feature, courses are offered to global learners with diverse backgrounds and cultures. This research has conducted a systematic literature review to identify the cultural aspects of multicultural learning environments and MOOCs, and what strategies, approaches, and dimensions have been implemented to deal with cultural challenges in relation to learning and teaching. The results showed how cultural differences on many levels are an influential factor on learning and teaching. Several pedagogical, contextual, and behavioural strategies have been implemented to overcome cultural differences in learning. In conclusion, this report presents an inventory of suggestions for a MOOC development team to consider when they are designing and delivering MOOC courses for multicultural audiences.

Keywords: massive open online courses, MOOC, multicultural, cultural challenges, systematic, literature review.

1. University of Southampton, Southampton, England; rs3c16@soton.ac.uk; https://orcid.org/0000-0002-7998-2304

2. University of Southampton, Southampton, England; hcd@soton.ac.uk; http://orcid.org/0000-0002-1182-1459

3. University of Southampton, Southampton, England; k.borthwick@soton.ac.uk; https://orcid.org/0000-0003-2251-7898

How to cite this chapter: Shahini, R., Davis, H. C., & Borthwick, K. (2019). Design recommendations to address cultural issues in multicultural MOOCs: a systematic literature review. In A. Plutino, K. Borthwick & E. Corradini (Eds), *New educational landscapes: innovative perspectives in language learning and technology* (pp. 55-62). Research-publishing.net. https://doi.org/10.14705/rpnet.2019.36.956

1. Introduction

MOOCs held the promise of democratising education and benefitting learners from diverse global backgrounds and cultures on a massive scale. However, they fail to manage culturally diverse learners' understanding, perceptions, and expectations (Dennen & Bong, 2018).

This research aimed to examine the importance of cultural differences from an educational perspective. It identified the gaps in research approaches and strategies regarding cultural issues in current MOOCs, and used the information learned to make some suggestions to facilitate globalisation in MOOC design.

Two research questions were defined to guide the research inquiry and these are mentioned in the *Results and discussion* section.

2. Method

This research carried out a systematic literature review of published literature about MOOCs between 2016 and 2018. It used an established procedure for systematic literature reviews in social sciences (Siddaway, 2014), which suggests six stages of reviewing: scoping; planning; identification; screening; eligibility; and performing quantitative and qualitative research synthesis.

Terms relating to the research questions were established, and initial searches were conducted using the keywords 'MOOC' or 'massive open online course' and 'culture' or 'culture*', to balance between getting as many papers as possible and ensuring the relevance of these papers. Only empirical studies were included.

The language was limited to English and filtered according to the availability of full text in these databases. Electronic databases were selected for use in the research according to their relevance to the focus of the topic and the scope (Scopus, Web of Science, Eric).

3. Results and discussion

3.1. RQ1 – How diverse are the cultural origins of online learning environments and MOOCs compared to the cultural origins and expectations of learners?

In order to examine cultural origins, we attempted to discover the country of origin and language of each of the MOOCs described in the literature. The results are shown in Figure 1 and Figure 2.

Figure 1. The cultural origins of MOOCs

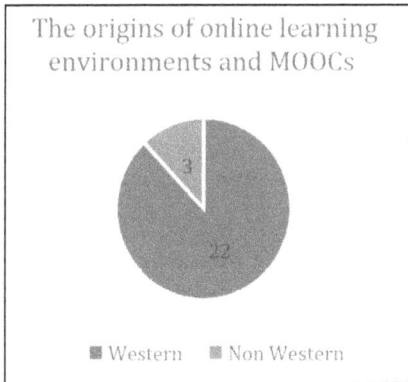

The origins of online learning environments and MOOCs

3

22

■ Western   ■ Non Western

Figure 2. The language of instruction in MOOCs

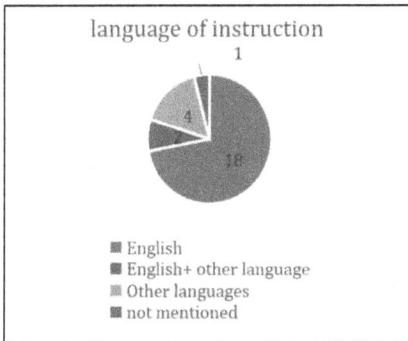

language of instruction

1

4

18

■ English
■ English+ other language
■ Other languages
■ not mentioned

The origins of the MOOC country were not always referred to. Therefore, the origins of platforms were classified according to the platform provider and the origin of the institution which constructed the course.

We can see that the majority of MOOCs originate from Western counties and are implemented primarily in English. These results are not surprising given that:

- MOOCs originally stemmed from the West;

- four out of five top MOOC providers in the world, according to enrolments, are Western (Shah, 2017);

- famous Western platforms have partnerships with top ranked universities, facilitating research on these platforms; and

- English is commonly the 'lingua franca' and a bridging language in global education.

It is challenging for learners from different cultures to fit in with the unfamiliar Western centric course design and execution. However, the majority of learners prefer to learn and communicate with diverse learners in English. It is important to go beyond language level into depth to resolve and design courses that support diverse cultures with different pedagogical needs.

3.2. RQ2 – What strategies have been applied in online learning environments and MOOCs to overcome cultural challenges in previous studies?

3.2.1. National or individual level of culture

The results of the literature survey identified a two-sided discussion in relation to cultural differences. On one side, more than half of the publications were exploring the effects of cultural differences on a *national* level. This research treats nationality as a proxy for the learner's culture and compares the experience of students from different countries (Che, Luo, Wang, & Meinel, 2016), and also looks at the experience of students who are from a different culture than the MOOC's origin when considering the content and services of the MOOC (Phan, 2018).

The other papers stressed the importance of investigating cultural differences on an *individual* level. Diversity in perception of MOOC content and activities are stemmed from the combined effect of the physical world, experiences, and course design influencing learners in various degrees. Expectations about the course and instructors significantly varies even with the same learning culture (Loizzo & Ertmer, 2016).

Culture is not equivalent to countries and nations; it has undetermined boundaries that have to be studied carefully in respect to different levels of culture and with consideration to the global nature of MOOCs that affect participants in various degrees.

3.2.2.   Internationalisation versus localisation

Analysing the literature sample, two approaches were identified to overcome cultural differences; *internationalisation* and *localisation* in multicultural learning environments.

On one hand, *internationalisation* as a discipline specific term refers to creating learning and assessment materials that incorporate international themes or perspectives (Mittelmeier et al., 2018).

It was supported by many studies such as Dennen and Bong (2018), and Bozkurt and Keefer (2017), and suggested that the following features can enrich the overall learning experience:

- implementing flexible content with multiple updated versions;

- opening the learning space for participation and editing; and

- offering variety of learning options and facilities.

On the other hand, the other literature proposed *localisation* of MOOCs to overcome cultural challenges by adapting content and services to suit a specific cultural characteristic (Krasny et al., 2018).

In the MOOC context, balancing between the two strategies can be pedagogically beneficial in overcoming cultural challenges. This suggested approach can be produced as a spectrum adjusted according to the nature of learning elements and inputs with efforts from both course designers and diverse learners.

4.   Conclusions and recommendations

In this paper we have shown that the 'one-size-fits-all' model does not work for multicultural environments. Using the results of the research above, we have derived the following recommendations for MOOC designers and facilitators, which we believe balance the different strategies to allow learners from multiple cultures to take control of and optimise their learning.

- Dynamic design: course design has to be changed and updated frequently (Dennen & Bong, 2018) as a substantial number of culturally diverse learners with different perceptions, expectations, and points of view join the course and can enrich the learning experience.

- Flexible pathways: give the learners control over their learning process by offering multiple culturally sensitive options that may match learners' cultural characteristics and their preferred learning culture.

- Flexible content: adjusting the content making it culturally relevant to learners' diverse local contexts and backgrounds as it boosts learners' engagement (Mittelmeier et al., 2018). Sophisticated concepts can be explained in multiple contexts. Developers are encouraged to adjust activities, assignments, and examples making them culturally related to learners' local worlds.

- MOOCs as an assemblage point: designers can enhance globalisation and multiculturality of MOOC courses by opening the learning space for participants to construct knowledge depending on their own lifeworld experiences, engaging instructors to support learners by managing and updating these spaces, and, in addition, provide several options of technological tools and services to attract a wider range of diverse learners.

- Adopting innovative pedagogical and instructional strategies such as personalised learning and context-based learning.

References

Bozkurt, A., & Keefer, J. (2017). Participatory learning culture and community formation in connectivist MOOCs. *Interactive Learning Environments, (December)*, 1-13. https://doi.org/10.1080/10494820.2017.1412988

Che, X., Luo, S., Wang, C., & Meinel, C. (2016). An Attempt at MOOC localization for Chinese-speaking users. *International Journal of Information and Education Technology, 6*(2), 90-96. https://doi.org/10.7763/IJIET.2016.V6.665

Dennen, V. P., & Bong, J. (2018). Cross-cultural dialogues in an open online course : navigating national and organizational cultural differences. *TechTrends, 62*(4), 383-392. https://doi.org/10.1007/s11528-018-0276-7

Krasny, M. E., DuBois, B., Adameit, M., Atiogbe, R., Alfakihuddin, M. L. B., Bold-erdene, T., & Shian-Yun, L. (2018). Small groups in a social learning MOOC (sIMOOC): strategies for fostering learning and knowledge creation. *Online Learning, 22*(2), 119-139. https://doi.org/10.24059/olj.v22i2.1339

Loizzo, J., & Ertmer, P. A. (2016). MOOCocracy: the learning culture of massive open online courses. *Educational Technology Research and Development, 64*(6), 1013-1032. https://doi.org/10.1007/s11423-016-9444-7

Mittelmeier, J., Rienties, B., Tempelaar, D., Hillaire, G., & Whitelock, D. (2018). The influence of internationalised versus local content on online intercultural collaboration in groups: a randomised control trial study in a statistics course. *Computers and Education, 118*(November 2017), 82-95. https://doi.org/10.1016/j.compedu.2017.11.003

Phan, T. (2018). Instructional strategies that respond to global learners' needs in massive open online courses. *Online Learning Journal, 22*(2), 95-118. https://doi.org/10.24059/olj.v22i2.1160

Shah, D. (2017). Class central learner survey (2017): MOOC users highly educated, have experienced career benefits — class central. https://www.class-central.com/report/class-central-learner-survey-2017/

Siddaway, A. (2014). What is a systematic literature review and how do I do one. *University of Stirling, 1*(Ii), 1-13.

9 The lights and shadows of intercultural exchange projects for 21st-century skills development: analysis and comparison of two online case studies

Marta Fondo[1] and Pedro Jacobetty[2]

Abstract

This study analyses the results of two parallel two-month online exchange projects launched during the spring semester of 2018. The first project was a bilingual one-to-one English/Spanish exchange project for undergraduate business students. The second one was a monolingual one-to-many intercultural practice in English between native and non-native undergraduate business/economics students. Whereas both projects followed a similar structure, they differed in many aspects. Our mixed-methods approach focusses on student profile, project and task design, implementation, and coordination, in relation to students' participation, performance, and their evaluation of the project. The objective is to identify what led to positive (lights) and negative (shadows) outcomes and to provide a collection of project design recommendations to telecollaboration practitioners.

Keywords: telecollaboration, project design, student perceptions.

1. Universitat Oberta de Catalunya, Barcelona, Spain; mfondo@uoc.edu; https://orcid.org/0000-0003-1181-2322

2. The University of Edinburgh, Edinburgh, Scotland; pjacobet@ed.ac.uk; https://orcid.org/0000-0002-0018-4749

How to cite this chapter: Fondo, M., & Jacobetty, P. (2019). The lights and shadows of intercultural exchange projects for 21st-century skills development: analysis and comparison of two online case studies. In A. Plutino, K. Borthwick & E. Corradini (Eds), *New educational landscapes: innovative perspectives in language learning and technology* (pp. 63-69). Research-publishing.net. https://doi.org/10.14705/rpnet.2019.36.957

1. Introduction

Since pedagogy tacked from teacher-centred to learner-centred approaches, learning has been seen as a process facilitated by the teacher and carried out by the learner (Lynch, 2010). The possibilities brought by the development of web 2.0 information and communication tools are nowadays playing a key role in supporting innovative teaching and learning practices (Lillejord, Børte, Nesje, & Ruud, 2018). An example is telecollaboration in education, that is, the use of computer and/or digital communication tools to promote learning through social interaction and collaboration among students (Dooly, 2017). However, as Jager, Kurek, and O'Rourke (2016) state, summarising David Little's contribution to their edited volume, "telecollaboration cannot by itself be an agent of fundamental change: it can only ever be as effective as the pedagogical environment it is embedded in" (p. 5). In the following sections, we analyse the project design features and student experiences in two telecollaboration projects. The objective is to better understand positive and negative effects of project design and implementation elements to inform future telecollaboration projects.

2. Method

The sample of this study comprised a total of 285 students:

- one-to-one bilingual (English/Spanish) exchange project: 89 students from Universitat Oberta de Catalunya (UOC), University of Minnesota (UMN), University of Maryland (UMBC), University of Limerick (UL), and Benemérita Universidad Autónoma de Puebla (BUAP); and

- one-to-many monolingual exchange project: 25 students from BUAP and 171 students from Queens College City University of New York (QCUNY).

The projects were part of the course assignments and were based on oral communication. The two projects ran synchronously and followed the same data gathering procedure differing only in the case of the QCUNY students, who did not participate in Foreign Language (FL) practice. For this reason, their questionnaires were adapted to cover only intercultural issues.

This paper is based on questionnaire data. The pre-project questionnaire sought to identify student profiles in terms of demographics and intercultural sensitivity levels. For the bilingual project, all the questionnaires were provided either in English or Spanish. Therefore, the intercultural sensitivity scale (Chen & Starosta, 2000) was translated into Spanish by the main researchers and a group of experts (see supplementary materials). Students' perceptions about tasks and interactions were gathered during every virtual exchange. Finally, their perception of the overall project and performance were measured using the Project Evaluation Questionnaire (PEQ).

3. Results and discussion

The dropout rate in both projects was low. The higher numbers of dropouts are among QCUNY students. Working in groups could have had a negative effect on the students (Table 1).

Table 1. Students' participation rates

Type of project	Institution	Sample	Participation		
Bilingual One-on-one	University	Enrolled	Active	Inactive	Dropout
	BUAP	2	2	0	0
	UL	19	17	2	1
	UMN	22	20	2	0
	UMBC	6	3	3	1
	UOC	40	30	10	0
Monolingual One-to-many	QCUNY	171	147	24	21
	BUAP	25	23	2	2

Student perceptions about the project, gathered with the PEQ, show that students enjoyed participating in the project and perceive their participation to have positive effects in communicative and intercultural skills development (Table 2).

QCUNY had lower percentages expressing positive effects than its counterparts, but still high.

Table 2. Intercultural skills development and enjoyment during the project perceived by the students (percentages of students who answered quite/very much)

Item	Eng	UOC	BUAP	QCUNY
Developing skills for communicating with other people	71%	63%	71%	66%
Developing skills for interacting with people from other cultures	77%	73%	71%	70%
Developing skills for understanding other cultures	71%	73%	81%	75%
Enjoy getting to know someone from a different culture	86%	93%	95%	76%
Enjoy interacting with your partner	88%	83%	83%	72%
Liking to learn with someone from a different culture	80%	87%	100%	73%

As QCUNY students showed lower levels of enjoyment, we analysed their responses to the open question *In your opinion, what are the most important elements to have a successful online intercultural exchange experience?* from the PEQ. The answers reflected issues in three areas (Table 3):

- project design: lack of alignment between the project and the subject;

- task design: need for clarity in task descriptions and aims; and

- language: communication problems due to a low FL proficiency level in Mexican students.

As reflected in students' perceptions about the project, the shadows are grouped in project design, task design, and language barriers. Although QCUNY students valued positively the opportunity to use statistics in real-life contexts, they perceived a lack of structure in some tasks and had difficulties carrying them out.

They felt that the language barrier with their Mexican partners had a negative impact. QCUNY students worked in groups and formed the largest contingent of students in the projects (n=171). This may have hindered the possibility of personalised support, which could have affected engagement and dropout rates. However, students in QCUNY showed high levels of enjoyment and valued their participation in the project positively. Thus, the interactive and affective dimensions seem to promote motivation and engagement, making up for project design flaws identified by the students.

Table 3. Responses of QCUNY students to the open question

Project design	"This was not an organized and coherent project"
	"I really did not have a good time, thought it was pointless"
	"I feel that the topic was not very relevant to us and the project probably could have been better coordinated"
Task design	"More organized. More individualized – questions were not always applicable to our topic"
	"I feel like the topic of our discussion didn't allow much room for any huge conversation to happen"
Language	"I did not feel it was very beneficial because of the language barrier between me and my partne"
	"Respectfully, language was a barrier"
	"Our partner from Mexico had difficulties expressing himself in English"

4. Conclusions

The main problem teachers face in telecollaboration projects is the lack of institutional support in very time-consuming projects (Guth, Helm, & O'Dowd, 2014). In addition to this, our study revealed the importance of both project and task design, and especially attentive coordination and personalised student support. Complementary language assistance must be included in the learning materials when the interaction is monolingual and one-to-many to avoid communication breakdowns. In these projects, success is normally measured by dropout and completion rates as well as skill development and knowledge acquisition. Such measurements of success are fundamental but following the latest stream of research in pedagogy that links learning with emotion, we claim that enjoyment should also be included as part of the equation to measure the success of telecollaboration projects. The fun component added to the tasks and social interaction (level of enjoyment) in the projects has shown to keep the students motivated as they value the experience positively despite the flaws in the design.

Acknowledgements

We would like to thank Schiro Withanachchi (QCUNY), Leticia Poblano (BUAP), and Laura Lamolla (UOC) for their support and collaboration.

Supplementary materials

https://research-publishing.box.com/s/q0s5ylm7lj3rb9nx5s02y1jjvjkq4hjk

References

Chen, G. M., & Starosta, W. J. (2000). The development and validation of the intercultural sensitivity scale. *Human Communication, 3*, 1-15.

Dooly, M. (2017). Telecollaboration. In C. A. Chapelle & S. Sauro (Eds), *The handbook of technology and second language teaching and learning* (pp. 169-183). John Wiley & Sons. https://doi.org/10.1002/9781118914069.ch12

Guth, S., Helm, F., & O'Dowd, R. (2014). Telecollaborative foreign language networks in European universities: a report on current attitudes and practices. *Bellaterra Journal of Teaching & Learning Language & Literature, 7*(4), 1-14. https://doi.org/10.5565/rev/jtl3.609

Jager, S., Kurek, M., & O'Rourke, B. (2016). New directions in telecollaborative research and practice: introduction. In S. Jager, M. Kurek & B. O'Rourke (Eds), *New directions in telecollaborative research and practice: selected papers from the second conference on telecollaboration in higher education* (pp. 1-15). Research-publishing.net. https://doi.org/10.14705/rpnet.2016.telecollab2016.486

Lillejord, S., Børte, K., Nesje, K., & Ruud, E. (2018). *Learning and teaching with technology in higher education – a systematic review*. Knowledge Centre for Education. www.kunnskapssenter.no

Lynch, D. N. (2010). *Student-centered learning: the approach that better benefits students*. Virginia Wesleyaan College.

10 Telecollaboration in the foundation year classroom: the 'Global Student Collective'

Lucy Watson[1]

Abstract

The 'Global Student Collective' is a telecollaboration project on the International Foundation Year (IFY) programme at the University of Southampton. IFY students were connected with volunteers in Brazil, India, Hungary, and Italy online in order to find out more about their countries. The project required the students to exercise multiple transferable skills, including teamwork, time management, and intercultural awareness. They also developed vital oral, written, and digital skills. The researcher used an Exploratory Practice (EP) approach utilising existing pedagogical activities for data collection. This paper identifies the challenges the project presented and presents preliminary findings from the research data in order to assist practitioners interested in telecollaboration to design their own projects.

Keywords: telecollaboration, global citizenship, intercultural competence, foundation year.

---

1. University of Southampton, Southampton, England; l.a.watson@soton.ac.uk

How to cite this chapter: Watson, L. (2019). Telecollaboration in the foundation year classroom: the 'Global Student Collective'. In A. Plutino, K. Borthwick & E. Corradini (Eds), *New educational landscapes: innovative perspectives in language learning and technology* (pp. 71-76). Research-publishing.net. https://doi.org/10.14705/rpnet.2019.36.958

---

1.   Introduction

This paper focusses on the 'Global Student Collective', a telecollaboration project which was introduced in October 2018 on the IFY programme at the University of Southampton, UK. The 17 IFY students were mixed-nationality, non-native speakers between 17-19 years old. Telecollaboration is a method of connecting people in different locations using digital technology to work collectively on a project (O'Dowd, 2018). The six week project was piloted on a compulsory module called 'Global Society'. This module introduces students to key concepts of global governance and economic structures and encourages them to explore contemporary issues, such as global warming, global inequality, migration, and human rights.

Increasingly, students need to develop the skills and knowledge to enter a globalised academic environment. This includes broadening their understanding of the world around them, their place within it, and helping them develop the communication and digital skills necessary to participate fully. A recent UKCISA (2018) report highlighted a gap in curriculum development with regard to global citizenship. The survey defined global citizenship as "being able to interact more freely and meaningfully with people of different nationalities and backgrounds" (UKCISA, 2018, p. 50). Global Society encourages students to view themselves as "'global citizen[s]' who [are] preparing to study at an outward-looking university with an international focus" (Edwards & Watson, 2017, n.p.). Building on previous work on global citizenship in education, the 'Global Student Collective' project was devised to connect IFY students with people from different backgrounds and with different perspectives, not just the 'mobile elite', which (arguably) they represent (Aktas, Pitts, Richards, & Silova, 2017; Andreotti, 2006; Rizvi, 2007; Shultz, 2007).

The 'Global Student Collective' connected the IFY students via a closed Facebook group with volunteer students from Brazil (postgraduates aged 21-24 studying biomedical sciences), India (postgraduates aged 21-23 studying political science), Hungary (undergraduate English majors, aged 19), and Italy (high school students, aged 16-18, from the same English class). The

IFY students gathered their opinions on their country's role and position in the world today and tried to discover more about the current economic, social, and political challenges facing those countries. The students collated the information and delivered a ten minute assessed group presentation on their findings, followed by a Q&A.

The final presentations were rich and nuanced and the student feedback was positive overall. Nevertheless, the cultural, educational, and age differences between the students presented some challenges. This paper will present the IFY students' reflections on the project and make suggestions for practitioners implementing telecollaboration projects themselves.

2.   Method

IFY students managed their interactions with their telecollaboration partners, and IFY tutor correspondence with the students abroad was limited. First, the IFY students made introductory videos and posted them on the Facebook group. The students from Brazil, India, Italy, and Hungary responded and the groups connected. They then decided how to communicate further.

The students were asked to shift their discussion focus over three themes: 'my country and me' (personal reflections on what their nationality means to them); 'my country in the world' (fact-based analysis of the economy and challenges facing their country); and 'me in the world' (their understanding of 'global citizenship'). This encouraged the students to move from general commentary about nationality and culture to more complex and controversial topics.

EP research techniques were used (Allwright, 2003). This involved utilising "normal pedagogic practices as investigative tools" (Allwright, 2003, p. 127), including a teacher diary, regular student feedback, and whole class discussions. The presentations and the Q&A also offered further insights. A questionnaire was also sent to all IFY students. Twelve out of 17 responded. Some of the main points from this combined research data are outlined below.

3.   Results and discussion

The nature and volume of communication between the groups differed. Seven of the questionnaire respondents reported they were in contact more than once a week, and nine agreed their students responded to their questions. However, four students reported they found it difficult to express themselves, possibly because of a lack of confidence or language ability. After initial introductions, most students continued corresponding through WhatsApp and Messenger. Two IFY students suggested using 'video' or 'facetime' would have helped communication, but none did so.

There were 27 Italian high school students and their form tutor guided the project. The IFY students adapted their approach accordingly and sent their questions in advance, which the Italians responded to in small groups. This resulted in fewer, more formal interactions focussed mainly on the objectives of the project.

Privacy concerns were raised and a letter was written in Italian to parents explaining the aims of the project and reassuring them that their children's information would not be shared. This supports O'Dowd's (2015) recommendation that the expectations of the groups of volunteers and their attitudes to social media as a teaching and learning tool should be considered. Furthermore, the IFY students noted that the Italian students might be 'a bit too young' to consider politics. Some preparation on the cultural contexts of the students would have been useful, helping the IFY students to develop their 'intercultural awareness' before the task.

In contrast, communication with the four Brazilians was lively and relaxed. The IFY students reported that they were in contact 'all the time, at least once a day'. When asked what they discussed, one student said "Anything! Movies, gaming, fashion, so many things. They are very friendly". The Brazilians were 21-23 years old and confident communicators. They did not study together so communication tended to be one-to-one. When asked how this was established, the IFY cohort explained that they chose each other 'naturally' as relationships developed. With politics, the Brazilians were concerned about 'upsetting' the others in the group and preferred to respond individually, acknowledging the sensitivity of the topic. Again, this highlights the importance of pre-work on intercultural awareness (Dooly, 2008).

The four Indians were political science Master's students and saw the project as an opportunity to educate the IFY students about India. When asked about the nature of their interactions, the IFY reported that they got a lot of facts but no 'feelings'. They said, "we tried to figure out their opinions from the language they were using". They learned from this saying, "next time we will aim to get their own opinions rather than pure information".

The four Hungarian students were less forthcoming and needed to be prompted by the IFY group. They seemed reluctant to talk about political issues. One Hungarian student was willing to, but not on a 'public' forum. At the time, Hungary was experiencing political upheaval (BBC, 2018) and tutors had discussed possible problems via email prior to the project. It was felt that participants may need "to acknowledge the limits [of] their interview questions in order to take local issues into account", further highlighting the importance of cultural awareness during telecollaboration.

Overall, the students enjoyed the project, citing the "amazing opportunity" to "do something different". One group said, "we learned about a new culture and a different lifestyle", and another said, "it is absolutely more interesting to talk to them than researching by yourself".

4.   Conclusions

The IFY students practised time management, teamwork, and digital communication skills during this telecollaboration project. Based on this project, key recommendations for fellow practitioners are: (1) ensure that sufficient time is devoted to the project and that expectations are clear, (2) enable face-to-face communication through videoconferencing, and (3) embed intercultural competence in the learning process.

Acknowledgements

Thanks to my colleague Elwyn Edwards for his support.

References

Allwright, D. (2003). Exploratory practice: rethinking practitioner research in language teaching. *Language Teaching Research, 7*(2), 113-141. https://doi.org/10.1191/1362168803lr118oa

Andreotti, V. (2006). Soft versus critical global citizenship education. *Policy and Practice, 3,* 40-51.

Aktas, F., Pitts, K., Richards, J. C., & Silova, I. (2017). Institutionalizing global citizenship: a critical analysis of higher education programs and curricula. *Journal of Studies in International Education, 21*(1), 65-80. https://doi.org/10.1177/1028315316669815

BBC. (2018, September 12). *EU parliament votes to punish Hungary over 'breaches' of core values.* https://www.bbc.co.uk/news/world-europe-45498514

Dooly, M. (2008). *Telecollaborative language learning: a guidebook to moderating intercultural collaboration online.* Peter Lang.

Edwards, E., & Watson, L. (2017). *Global society module specification.* https://www.southampton.ac.uk/courses/modules/ifyp0014.page

O'Dowd, R. (2015). The competences of the telecollaborative teacher. *The Language Learning Journal, 43*(2), 194-207. https://doi.org/10.1080/09571736.2013.853374

O'Dowd, R. (2018). From telecollaboration to virtual exchange: state-of-the-art and the role of UNICollaboration in moving forward. *Journal of Virtual Exchange, 1,* 1-23. Research-publishing.net. https://doi.org/10.14705/rpnet.2018.jve.1

Rizvi, F. (2007). Postcolonialism and Globalization in Education. *Cultural Studies ↔ Critical Methodologies, 7*(3), 256-263. https://doi.org/10.1177/1532708607303606

Shultz, L. (2007). Educating for global citizenship: conflicting agendas and understandings. *The Alberta Journal of Educational Research, 53*(3), 248-58.

UKCISA. (2018). *Pathways to success.* https://ukcisa.org.uk/resources_download.aspx?resourceid=171&documentid=284

11 What I did on my holidays: digital fieldtrips and digital literacies

Sarah Fielding[1]

Abstract

If a picture says a thousand words, how much can a 360°
image say? How can experiencing (or understanding) other
languages and cultures be conveyed in immersive experiences?
The Digital Learning Team at the University of Southampton has
been developing innovative resources whilst piloting the use of
Thinglink, a subscription- and browser-based software which allows
educators and students to create interactive 360° tours embedded
with rich media tags and online forms. As mentioned in Fielding
and Peel (2017), "[u]sually it takes months of training to develop a
virtual world but Thinglink allows this to be done in a short space
of time by users with no previous experience" (n.p.). Students could
develop digital literacies and skills by creating immersive narratives
of their experiences beyond the university environment. In exploring
one easy to apply production process, we are at an early stage of
innovative practice which has applications for many disciplines.
This report outlines aspects of our production process and gives top
tips for designing for 360° resources.

Keywords: immersive, digital, 360°, virtual.

1. University of Southampton, Southampton, England; s.fielding@soton.ac.uk

How to cite this chapter: Fielding, S. (2019). What I did on my holidays: digital fieldtrips and digital literacies. In A. Plutino, K. Borthwick & E. Corradini (Eds), *New educational landscapes: innovative perspectives in language learning and technology* (pp. 77-83). Research-publishing.net. https://doi.org/10.14705/rpnet.2019.36.959

1.   Introduction

Mixed reality, including virtual and augmented realities, is identified in the 2018 New Media Consortium New Horizon report (Becker et al., 2018) as having a "time to adoption" timeframe of four to five years (p. 46). The field is evolving rapidly, with technology for capture, creation, and deployment becoming more affordable, efficient, and effective. Virtual platforms allow individuals to explore environments and discover and investigate at their own pace (Cameron et al., 2005). The body of literature is also developing rapidly with growing evidence that immersive experiences confer various benefits to learning. These include increased engagement (de Freitas et al., 2010), a sense of telepresence in otherwise rarely or inaccessible environments (Schultze, 2014), and enhanced recall of environmental context-dependant memories (Jahn et al., 2018).

Although mixed reality technology is becoming more mainstream and accessible, it is still underused in the majority of higher education teaching. More familiar to faculty staff and students are 360° immersive experiences, accessed via platforms such as Google Earth, StreetView, and bespoke virtual campus tours. These are usually passively consumed, or outsourced to external providers with the necessary skills and software to produce. However, Thinglink (a browser-based subscription model software) is a tool which allows educators and students alike to create interactive 360° tours embedded with rich media tags and online forms.

2.   Production process

Whilst the platforms which can host the resource vary in terms of functionality and user experience, the production process is less variable: 360° image capture, embedded media capture, asset list/storyboard, and uploading into editing software.

2.1.   Storyboarding and image creation

A storyboard (either a Word or Excel file) is part of the planning process and an important part of recording copyright permissions. It should contain links to any embedded materials published elsewhere online, images used to indicate hotspots and for more detailed notes of bespoke materials created for the resource, such as contributors, release forms, etc.

360° image capture is possible using multiple-lens cameras, or by using iOS or Android apps (although these will sometimes require post-production editing). The positioning of the camera has a significant impact on the user's experience; it should be located in a natural position of a person, at an appropriate average human height, and carefully aligned so that the 'seams' of the lenses do not cut across faces or features of interest in the environment. Logos and creation credits can be used in post-production to disguise unwanted elements of the image. A further option in Thinglink is to clone images that have been uploaded by other users, but are not explicitly licensed under Creative Commons.

2.2.   Embedded rich media tags

Embedded media in Thinglink can include, but is not limited to; audio recordings, videos, images, online forms or surveys, and other websites. Whilst the learner has greater personal agency in exploring a 360° image, they can also benefit from some general guidance in using the resource. An introductory hotspot, identified with a 'start here' icon, describes what is available in the resource and any learning outcomes, and is a useful anchor. The nature of the hotspots contributes to the richness of the environment; a resource in which the user passively consumes content is less engaging than the opportunity to demonstrate new knowledge via virtual whiteboards, forms, and social media hashtags.

Embedding some form of providing feedback on the resource (such as a poll, form, or survey) will enable future improvements. When designing a tour that includes multiple locations linked together, use transition icons and labels consistently so that learners don't become disoriented. For example, all transition icons in a resource are green circles with a white directional arrow, and labels read 'Go back to X' (Figure 1). Large tours can quickly become tiresome to navigate through, so it is useful to add a 'Teleport' icon which will transition the user back to the home, or starting, image.

Figure 1.   The Thinglink editing interface

3.   Pedagogical benefits of 360° resources

The pedagogical benefits of this new medium (360° experiences, not limited to Thinglink) in higher education are relatively unexplored. Initial studies such as Walshe, Driver, Jakes, and Winstanley (2019) indicate improved personal reflection and more nuanced understanding of decision making and *in situ* responses for trainee teachers. In the same summary, Walshe et al. (2019) note the importance of "spatial situatedness, as students feel as though they are physically in the classroom when engaging with the 360°-degree experiences" (n.p.). The embodied feeling of 'being there' (Heidegger, 1962) adds to the authenticity of the experience and allows for deeper learning.

Going beyond functional information technology skills, the digital capability of an individual encompasses media literacies, communication, problem solving, and even wellbeing in online environments (JISC, n.d.). There are numerous applications for this type of context-based, situational learning resource in higher education:

- making previously inaccessible (or rarely accessible) environments available, such as clinical settings with patients;

- annotations to increase vocabulary;

- year abroad pre-activities to get to know Erasmus partner university towns/environment;

- specific scenes could contribute to the development of language for specific purposes;

- provide rich personal narratives from a learner perspective to reduce sense of isolation in new cohorts; and

- reducing anxiety levels in some students by aligning expectations of upcoming learning experiences, such as placements or assessments.

Figure 2.   The SAMR model[2]

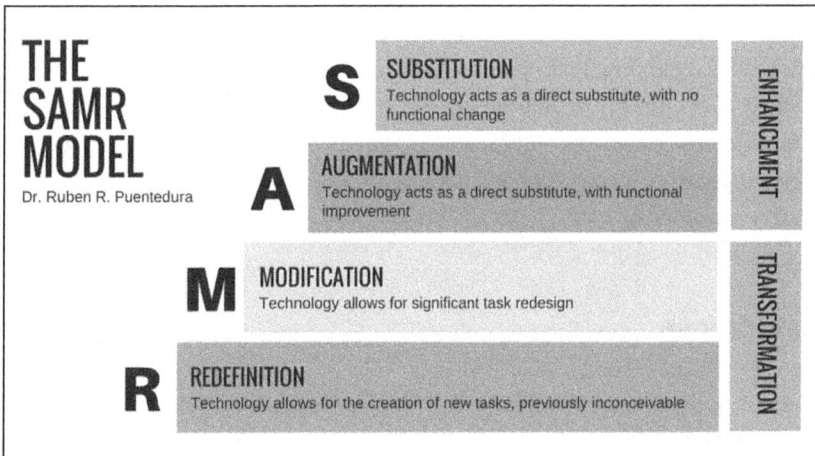

THE SAMR MODEL
Dr. Ruben R. Puentedura

S SUBSTITUTION
Technology acts as a direct substitute, with no functional change

A AUGMENTATION
Technology acts as a direct substitute, with functional improvement

ENHANCEMENT

M MODIFICATION
Technology allows for significant task redesign

R REDEFINITION
Technology allows for the creation of new tasks, previously inconceivable

TRANSFORMATION

2. By Lefflerd, CC BY-SA 4.0: https://commons.wikimedia.org/w/index.php?curid=47961924

Educators can develop the digital capabilities of their students by designing activities in which learners use Thinglink to create their own interactive virtual tours. This type of task could simultaneously improve lower levels of Bloom's (1956) taxonomy, such as recall by providing more engaging knowledge checks or quizzes, whilst allowing students to develop upper level skills such as creating new resources. In combination with Bloom's (1956) taxonomy and the Substitution, Augmentation, Modification, and Redefinition (SAMR) model for the use of technology in education (Puentedura, 2013) shown in Figure 2 above, Thinglink has the potential for students to achieve much deeper learning through the process of creating their own resources.

4.   Conclusion and future work

The use of immersive media will become more commonplace in higher education settings (Becker et al., 2018). Reduced costs and improved tools mean that staff and students are more enabled to create their own resources. This in turn can make placements more inclusive, provide opportunities for novel revision material and assessment, and further democratise access and learning.

The Digital Learning Team will continue to pilot the use of Thinglink as well as other tools for developing immersive learning experiences created for, and with, students. Phase one feedback is expected in the current academic year for pilot resources, and phase two includes co-creation of resources with students in various disciplines.

References

Becker, S. A., Brown, M., Dahlstrom, E., Davis, A., DePaul, K., Diaz, V., & Pomerantz, J. (2018). *NMC Horizon report: 2018 higher education edition*. EDUCAUSE. https://library.educause.edu/~/media/files/library/2018/8/2018horizonreport.pdf

Bloom, B. S. (1956). *Taxonomy of educational objectives, handbook I: the cognitive domain*. David McKay Co Inc.

Cameron, I. T., Crosthwaite, C. A., Donaldson, A., Samsudi, H., & Fry, M. (2005). *An immersive learning environment for process engineering using real VR.* CHEMECA Conference (Sept). Brisbane.

De Freitas, S., Rebolledo-Mendez, G., Liarokapis, F., Magoulas, G., & Poulovassilis, A. (2010). Learning as immersive experiences: using the four-dimensional framework for designing and evaluating immersive learning experiences in a virtual world. *British Journal of Educational Technology, 41*(1). 69-85. https://doi.org/10.1111/j.1467-8535.2009.01024.x

Fielding, S., & Peel, D. (2017). *Virtually there; a Thinglink approach to developing immersive experiences.* Association for learning technology. https://altc.alt.ac.uk/2017/sessions/virtually-there-a-thinglink-approach-to-developing-immersive-experiences-1833/members/

Heidegger, M. (1962). *Being and time.* Harper and Row.

Jahn, K., Kampling, H., Klein, H. C., Kuru, Y., & Niehaves, B. (2018). *Towards an explanatory design theory for context-dependent learning in immersive virtual reality.* PACIS 2018 Proceedings, 235. https://aisel.aisnet.org/pacis2018/235

JISC. (n.d.). *What is digital capability?* https://digitalcapability.jisc.ac.uk/what-is-digital-capability/

Puentedura, R. R. (2013). *SAMR: moving from enhancement to transformation.* http://www.hippasus.com/rrpweblog/archives/000095.html

Schultze, U. (2014). Performing embodied identity in virtual worlds. *European Journal of Information Systems, 23*(1), 84-95. https://doi.org/10.1111/j.1467-8535.2009.01024.x

Walshe, N., Driver, P., Jakes, T., & Winstanley, J.-M. (2019). *Developing trainee teacher understanding of pedagogy and practice using 360 degree video and an interactive digital overlay.* https://impact.chartered.college/article/developing-trainee-teacher-understanding-pedagogy-practice-using-360-degree-video-interactive-digital-overlay/

12 "What is this place?" – using screencasts to guide international students around the virtual learning environment

Michael Salmon[1]

Abstract

When using Virtual Learning Environments (VLEs) on university modules, international students unfamiliar with such platforms face navigational as well as linguistic barriers. Short, intensive language courses may not spend time on VLE orientation and rationale, with the result that students do not receive clear guidance on exactly how to move around the site, and why. This paper presents a narrative account of a teaching and site design intervention which used screencast videos to show students narrated examples of page navigation. These screencasts could be accessed multiple times and were not limited to an induction phase of the course. Take-up of these screencasts was high, and reported problems with VLE navigation reduced.

Keywords: VLE, screencasting, international students, pre-sessional.

1. Introduction

Pre-sessional language courses are offered to prospective university students who have not met the language proficiency requirements of their degree programmes, often in an intensive six or ten week format. Due to this intensity and short duration, teaching students how to make best use of a VLE may not

1. University of Liverpool in London, London, England; m.salmon@liverpool.ac.uk; https://orcid.org/0000-0003-2160-4076

How to cite this chapter: Salmon, M. (2019). "What is this place?" – using screencasts to guide international students around the virtual learning environment. In A. Plutino, K. Borthwick & E. Corradini (Eds), *New educational landscapes: innovative perspectives in language learning and technology* (pp. 85-90). Research-publishing.net. https://doi.org/10.14705/rpnet.2019.36.960

be a priority for the course designers, and students might be reluctant to spend time "learning how to learn" (Mitchell, Stephens, & Cook, 2006, p. 74). On the other hand, pre-sessional courses at many institutions are huge endeavours with a large team of tutors and technicians involved, and the value of a VLE for coordination and communication has been commented on in a UK higher education setting (e.g. Read, 2016).

This paper will focus on a pre-sessional course in which the students were exclusively from China, and draw on literature relating to attitudes towards VLE usage from Chinese learners. Nevertheless, much of the below will be relevant to international students more generally, and to the principles of good VLE design.

Studies (e.g. Chen, Bennett, & Maton, 2008) have shown that for Chinese learners new to higher education in another geographical context, the use of a VLE can seem 'doubly foreign', in that both the confrontation with technical language and the practice of navigating around an educational webpage specific to a module are new experiences. However, it is also important to note that students from China, and international students more widely, benefit from the use of VLEs as a form of learning which is "away from real-time communication", meaning that "the barriers of being embarrassed or being shy are partially removed" (Thompson & Ku, 2005, p. 35).

With these concerns in mind, this paper outlines a strategy for reducing the navigational barriers that VLEs can pose to international students unfamiliar with the online learning environments adopted in UK universities. This is based on a design approach taken on the University of Liverpool in London's pre-sessional course in 2018.

2. Approach

The use of video in a VLE has already been noted as a way to bring course content material alive (e.g. Hill & Nelson, 2011) due to its nature of a visual, kinetic medium as opposed to text or static image. In this teaching intervention, however, and in light of the navigational barriers remarked on above, it was decided to utilise videos for the objective of orienting students, rather than for content delivery. To be specific, on many VLE pages a video was placed to show students how to navigate the page and explain the usefulness of the content.

These videos were screencasts of the page being used, meaning that students could watch where to click or move the cursor, while listening to the module co-ordinator explain the resource, give advice on its usage, and gloss its role in the course and relationship to other resources. Figure 1 below is an example of this. The resource in question is a link to a reading list for the course and it is accompanied by an embedded video. On playing the video, the students are shown a live example of someone navigating the reading list, commenting on the material, opening the links, etc. This offers much more detailed guidance on using the resource than the alternatives of (1) simply including a link to the resource or (2) including a link to the resource with a description or static screenshots. The kinetic nature of video is more engaging for students, less cluttered on the screen, and tackles the barrier often faced by international students of not knowing how to navigate VLE pages.

Figure 1.   Example VLE screencast, reading list resource[2]

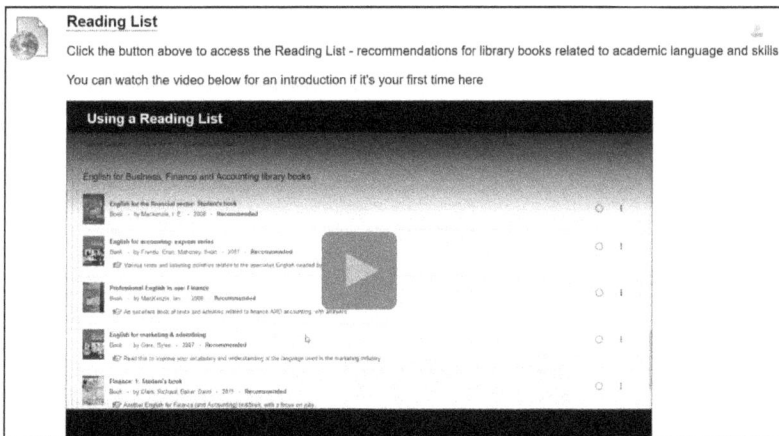

2. Screenshot, University of Liverpool in London pre-sessional VLE (Blackboard)

It has been remarked that VLE design is often institutional rather than course-specific (Ellaway, Dewhurst, & McLeod, 2004), meaning that the contents are set by policies outside the control of the module coordinators. The use of screencasts is a way to make the page more relatable for the students as the videos are specific to one particular course and linked (by voice) to familiar tutors. As learning objects, these screencasts are perhaps 'disposable' in the sense that they are designed specifically for one course's VLE, and would look out of place or incorrect if re-used. This requires more time, but means that the objects can be designed more carefully (Cheal & Rajagopalan, 2007, p. 68). Figure 2 is a screencast which was used to show students exactly how to navigate the Turnitin[3] submission for one particular assignment, and therefore which could not be re-used – the converse of this is that various concrete recommendations and reminders could be included, which would not be possible on a generic 'how to use Turnitin' non-screencast video.

Figure 2.   Example VLE screencast, report submission[4]

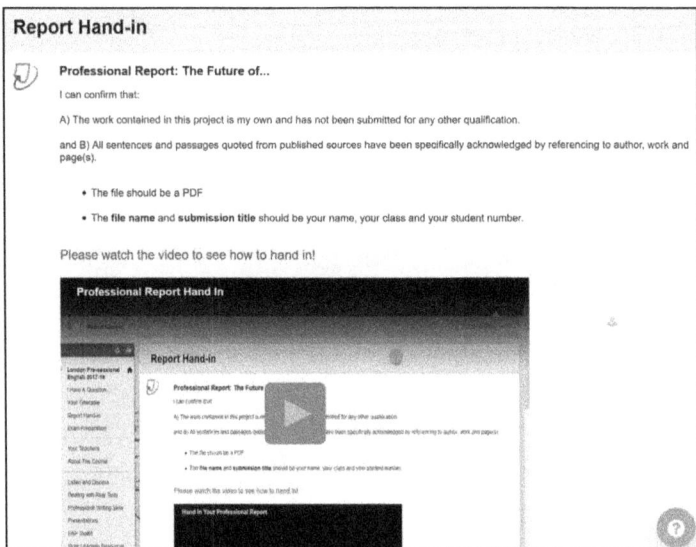

---

3. https://www.turnitin.com/

4. Screenshot, University of Liverpool in London pre-sessional VLE (Blackboard)

---

3.   Results and discussion

Table 1 shows the number of views of a selection of screencasts made available on the VLE. There was a cohort of 51 students on this course, so we can conclude that many screencasts were viewed multiple times by a large proportion of the students. However, it should be noted that the view count also includes tutors who might have watched the screencast, and that these figures do not necessarily reflect the video being viewed in its entirety.

Table 1.   View count for screencast videos

Resource/Feature	Number of views of screencast showing how to navigate the resource
Turnitin hand-in	445
Learning on screen	509
The academic word list	449
Accessing the Financial Times	208
How to access TED Talks	148
Using Quizlet	210
Task on Blackboard discussion board	566

Here are some of the observed benefits of using screencasts in this way:

- Better navigation on the page: as remarked above, international students in an unfamiliar education setting can fall back on narrated guides to know how and why the resources should be used.

- Reduced 'troubleshooting': the video guides save time spent instructing students on how to use the pages. For instance, all submissions to Turnitin were made without issues, which can otherwise be a source of stress at the deadline.

- Increased personalisation: through narration and specificity of content, the students are left in little doubt that the resources available on the VLE have been precisely selected for them and their context.

4.   Conclusions

Using narrated screencasts to help orient students who are unfamiliar with how VLEs are used by an institution proved an interesting way to present resources to students and guide and encourage their effective use, and this technique is certainly worthy of more investigation. In particular, gathering more qualitative feedback on student responses will be a logical next step, as the above intervention was done quite informally and relies on simple view counts and anecdotal evidence of efficacy.

References

Cheal, C., & Rajagopalan, B. (2007). A taxonomy showing relationships between digital learning objects and instructional design. In A. Koohang & K. Harman (Eds), *Learning objects and instructional design* (pp. 59-88). Informing Science Press.

Chen R. T.-H., Bennett, S., & Maton, K. (2008). The adaptation of Chinese international students to online flexible learning: two case studies. *Distance Education, 29*(3), 307-323. https://doi.org/10.1080/01587910802395821

Ellaway, R., Dewhurst, D., & McLeod, H. (2004). Evaluating a virtual learning environment in the context of its community of practice. *ALT-J, 12*(2), 125-145. https://doi.org/10.1080/0968776042000216192

Hill, J., & Nelson, M. (2011). Evaluating the perceived effectiveness of video podcasts as a learning resource for geography. *Planet, 24*(1), 76-82. https://doi.org/10.11120/plan.2011.00240076

Mitchell, P., Stephens, C., & Cook, A. (2006). E-tutor support for inducting distance-learning students. In A. Cook, K. A. Macintosh & B. S. Rushton (Eds), *Supporting students: early induction* (pp. 73-90). University of Ulster Press.

Read, D. (2016). Using technology to manage a pre-sessional: part 1 – managing information. http://learningtechnologiesineap.org/using-technology-to-manage-a-pre-sessional-part-1-managing-information/

Thompson, L., & Ku, H. (2005). Chinese graduate students' experience and attitudes toward online learning. *Educational Media International, 42*(1) 33-47. https://doi.org/10.1080/09523980500116878

Author index

A

Athanasiou, Androulla vi, 25

B

Borthwick, Kate v, 1, 55
Brick, Billy vi, 5

C

Cerveró Carrascosa, Abraham vi, 47
Cervi-Wilson, Tiziana vi, 5
Comas-Quinn, Anna vi, 41
Corradini, Erika v, 1

D

Davis, Hugh C. vii, 55

F

Fielding, Sarah vii, 77
Fondo, Marta vii, 63

G

Godson, Nina vii, 5
Graham, Sean vii, 5

J

Jacobetty, Pedro viii, 63

L

Loizou, Michael viii, 5

M

Markanastasakis, Christina viii, 19
Meri-Yilan, Serpil viii, 11

O

Orsini-Jones, Marina viii, 47

P

Papadima-Sophocleous, Salomi ix, 25

P

Pardoel, Bart ix, 25
Plutino, Alessia v, 1

R

Ryan, Kelly ix, 5

S

Salmon, Michael ix, 85
Shahini, Rana ix, 55

T

Tsankov, Tsvetan ix, 5

W

Watson, Lucy x, 71

Z

Zipf, Jessica x, 33